Vukulu Sizwe Maphindani

MESSAGE TO A
BLACKMAN
IN AFRICA

If My Yesterday offends my today, then it means there
is something wrong with my yesterday

SECOND EDITION

ISBN 13 :978-0-620-69971-6

First Published by Classic Age Publishing in 2015.
Second Impression : 2016
Third Impression : March 2017
Fourth Impression : June 2017
Po Box 134, Braamfontein, South Africa, 2001.

Cover Design by Classic Age Publishing
Website : www.classicagepublishing.co.za
Email : info@classicagepublishing.co.za

"You Are a Slave to your rent, your gas bill and telephone bill, a slave to your electricity and water bill, a slave to your job and tax bill; You are a slave!"

— Dr. Khalid Muhamad

Warning: this is not a book, but a letter, a message to Black people, this is the most thought provoking truth!

CONTENTS

ACKNOWLEDGEMENTS

MANY THANKS to Mr. Phala, a man who linearly unbolted my then entrapped curiosity with relation to black symbiosis in universal socio and economic relativity through his Black Nationalist teachings and his passion, determination, and personal delinquency to influence the trajectory of Black power dynamics in a democractic manifesting state as this one. He also, in only a few of our casual encounters abetted me to recognize, realize and honor Ancient African history and the importance of reminding Africans of the greater role they have played in the civilization of mankind; since history have ignored the role that the blackman has played in the development of mankind therefore kidnapping the psychological manifestation of self-determination in Black people.

I extend my unconditional Appreciation and acknowledgements to Dannie Adendorff and Manuela Cardiga of WDA Publishing, UK, for working with me in the first edition of this book. Especially that a writing of this rank is underpinned and censored by those who have been in control of the information in this rapidly floating Rainbow State; because the Blackman is the public enemy number 1. I appreciate Winston Maphindani [My father], Josephine Maphindani [My Mother], Johannes, Muhluri, and Muponisi Maphindani [All my brothers] for playing a foreseeable role in my life; and through these bloodlines, I'm conscious, vicious, confident, courageous and self-acknowledging of myself as a human being and as a Blackman in the face of a hostile social contract. I appreciate my sister in law, Nditsheni Joyce Maphindani for encouraging me and believing in me when no one else believed in me.

I appreciate Palesa Shiburi, My fiancé, for being with me, believing in me, encouraging me, standing with me, walking with me and fighting alongside me during my dark days. This message is also dedicated to my little daughter, Rhandzu Azania Maphindani, who will be growing in a society as rotten and dictious as this one.

INTRODUCTION

This book is an extension of the first edition which was written five years ago under docile circumstances in my development as a young Blackman growing in a Black Continent which is grappling with post modernity and colonial denominations or Colonial after effects. This is a doctrine of the African social rebellion against psychological warfare; it defies conventional thinking with an open argument which is equally critical to prod, provokes and enigmatically challenges the courage of the African mental ecosystem that has suffered the injustices of colonial victimization, incarceration, castration, indoctrinations, dehumanization and a psychological low-class alienation because Africans; like all other races are psychologically enabled and ideologically fit to play a major role in human civilization like they have proved the former back during the dark age and before colonialism with the introduction of the Tablet writing systems, Astrology, Architecture, Mathematics, fishing, building structures, early scientific education, steel, Coins, letters, Jewelleries and many inventions which later enticed the West to Invade Africa for numerous reasons, which ended up with some western felons developing ample jealous, ferocity and hate to rape the continent Africa by colonizing it. A human mind can achieve a millenium when working under no psychological entrapment. This book is a confrontational project, since it surveys the thought pattern Black power dynamics and re-education of centuries of miseducation that have been excuted to the Black mind causing a post-modern cosmological disorder. This book is one of many Melanin activating substances; and when black people's melanin substance is re-activated, we are rest assured that our native Self shall come together as Kings and Queens in harmony and peace like we have always been in the earliest days. And that's what you are; Kings and Queens. But what went wrong?

This message shall remain nothing new but rather a unique narrative in contextual development; and determined to provoke, inspire and educate the Blackman (refers to both Male and female Blacks). Since the teachings of Pan Africanism and Black Nationalism have always been interjected by westernisation because they have been in control of many African countries and are anxious of a cooperative Africa and Melanin-activated Black people. Since Africans' unity will fracture their capital gains; hence, they undercut Black Consciousness as a hate and racist teaching whilst reality tells that any race that takes pride in their own native self reflect patriotism.

The Blackman has suffered far too long, and there is no way that such a racial ordeal can be healed without mind, social, educational, economic, political, scientific, technological and industrial doctors. So, perceive this book as a mind, psychological and social doctor and treat it as such. I am not advocating for the revulsion of the Whiteman, but I'm narrating this message to play part in the re-education of the Black family into Melanin-reactivated Africans.

First, what is Melanin? In his book, Melanin – What Makes Black People Black, L. Africa defines Melanin as the biochemical substance that drives physical, mental, emotional and spiritual life. Melanin is an organic dark carbon chemical pigment substance; it gives Black people's eyes iris a brown color and give the dark color to their hair, skin and the Substantia Nigra of the brain. So, it is then believed that a people who possess Melanin are by nature pyscho-biologically superior. Therefore, it is relevant or rather necessary for the Black peoples of the world to learn and know the true knowledge of themselves in order to re-activate their natural superpowers!

You need to read, read, and read; because there is no man in the planet who can enslave a well-read brain. Wear less, but read more and you will become rich; because expensive clothes will soon wear out but information will forever remain

CHAPTER ONE

TO WHOM IT MAY CONCERN

I'M A STUDENT of Garveyism, a theological ideology which was preached and practiced by Marcus Garvey and I as such believe that the voice of Marcus Garvey is the voice that any human being in the world should hear from; particularly the Blackman, who has suffered the injustices of worldwide oppression, humiliation, exploitation, dehumanization, genocide, castration, social degradation, bloodshed, capitalism, slavery, slave labor, Public disobedience; Cultural, racial and psychological rape; destruction, incarceration and disaggregation. And like those who came before us said; wherever you go throughout the world, the "Blackman" is relegated to lower things; both economical and socially. Africa, the continent's original name was Alkabulan or Ethiopia (although this succinctly hold a continous debate); long before Southern Africa, colonization and the Slave-trade. It was dubbed and defined as Africa after a defeat by a Roman Warrior named ScipioAfricanus (this i according to many history sources), who fought with parts of North and Central Africa since they were the only parts of Africa back in the 2nd century. And as much as Western media have arrogated Africa as a home of barbarians and filthy cannibals who danced with monkeys before colonization and slavery; history then tells that the earliest civilization of mankind began in Africa, and there is nowhere in the history of man where Africans sing and dance with monkeys. That fraud was "lab created" for you to develop the idea of inferiority in your development; so, you must let go of that fairy-tale and vest yourself in truth, because the truth shall set you and the entire human family interested in racial justice free. We discovered our natural resources long before they came, and proof is, during the Dark Age, Mansa Musa [The King of Mali in the 1300c] was the richest man in the planet owning half of the world's gold, and when he visited Egypt on his religious pilgrimage to Mecca, he gave away massive gold to the Egyptian economy that crippled the economy of Egypt because he overweighed their economy with his colossal gold and wealth. He may be the richest of all times, owning gold that equaled 400 billion US Dollars.

So, today, all these is hidden; our history has become a fairy-tale in the eyes of the Black Family and the world, because Europe and the entire Anglo world didn't only colonize your resources, but they also took away your mind and kept the former in psychological imprisonement so that you can think exactly as they would want you to and you are doing exactly that. So it then makes sense that whenever any Black person reveals the original history of Africa as opposed to the fabricated fairy tale that is taught in schools (that in which shows parts of Africa only after colonization and reflect Africa as a backward continent before colonization) he is regarded as a traitor. When any Black Person commits to discerning the original unbiased truth about Africa he will, therefore, be regarded as a hate teacher or racist. Hence, the West and America have a problem with Black Power extremism and Black Consciousness.

What's offensive about one taking pride in their racial identity by vowing to stay conscious of his own self, surroundings and who he is as a human being? Why should that be unpleasant? And even to talk about the black genocide as fulfilled upon our people during colonization and in post colonialism is not commemorated anywhere in the world; because they believe we are as good as monkeys! The Jewish genocide as extremely actioned by Adolf Hitler is publicized everywhere in the world and even in some Museums in Africa. But as for the African genocide that involved more than a trillion lives lost during the 400-500 years of colonization, slavery and racial entrapment is not publicised nor acknowledged anywhere in the world, not even in Africa. Africa is sought to be independent, but 14 countries in Africa pay colonial tax to France. There are African countries that do not control their economies but are economically controlled by the preceding imperialist well-thought-out perpetual systems.

And a paramount understanding of my position in all of this will be appreciated. First, I don't hate white people, what I hate, contest and undermine is White Supremacy – there is a difference. Secondly, what is White Supremacy? White Supremacy is a scientific concept in White racism. Scientific Racism is the pseudoscientific study of techniques and hypotheses in order to support or justify the belief in racism, racial inferiority, or racial superiority; alternatively, it is the practice of classifying individuals of different phenotypes or genotypes into discrete races. Historically, it received credence in the scientific community led by Caucasians who racially profiled themselves as SUPERIOR to Black people using some hypocritical conclusions and analogies to justify their superiority by Black lashing Black people. Scientific racism employs anthropology (notably physical anthropology), anthropometry, craniometry, and other disciplines or pseudo-disciplines, in proposing anthropological typologies supporting the classification of human populations into physically discrete human races, that might be asserted to be superior or inferior. I, in a linear argument, and based on present day realities, believes that the Blackman is nowhere near freedom. Why should the Blackman, therefore, believes that he is free from colonial domination when the west and some parts of America still control his natural resources? Do you call it freedom when a leader like Thomas Sankara of Burkina Faso (Land of the upright man) has been slaughtered in cold blood for urging their people to consume what they produce and shouldn't be dependent to foreign trade? Do you call it freedom when a leader like MuammarAl-Gadhafi of Libya get assassinated for controlling his people's oil by refusing to trade in US dollars and also for selling same at credible, reasonable and qualitative price without disenchanted discounts? Gadafi urged Africa to come together and form the United States of Africa by backing the African currency with the mineral wealth. The idea of a United States Of Africa is not new, it first discussed by Marcus Garvey in the 1920's and then recited by Kwame Nkrumah in the 1950's. Do you call it independence when countries like Zimbabwe and the Democratic Republic of Congo are taken out of foreign trade by the White Power structure because of claiming back their land from colonial dispossession?

If you call it independence I think you are too comfortable with the material conspiracy against your black self. I call it the independence of the "African Political Elite" in the expense of the ordinary suffering BLACK majorities. Hence, in many countries, those who know the truth are fighting with all their might to become a "Political elite" in order to share the profits made by the "economic elite" who to this day remain corporates and State resource Nativists. Many African governments' claim to be what they call "A democratic government" which means a transparent government, but their economies are privately owned which becomes a contradiction of the supreme law.

You will be staggered on why many African swashbucklers are so eager to become statesmen or presidents in their respective countries, that they even kill the innocent in such an exertion because they have realized that it is only when you are a supreme leader of your government that you can become "A political elite".

Only then do you receive the smaller margins of the profits made from the exploitation of state resources and the bloodsucking of poor black men and women by the preceding imperialist enterprises, doctrines, systems and schemes aimed at individuality and public "mind control".

And to come together we also don't need protest. I don't believe in the concept of protest; it reflects weakness and lack of ingenuity, we have protested for over 400 years and it didn't work and so I believe that our processes of achieving what we really want (Black Power) should be a little ingenious and scientific. When you protest, you have no ammunition to achieve power but rather to attract clueless cloned Men in Blue who will shoot and kill some of you whilst your response may be burning your own property which is relevant to your Black community and how do you challenge White supremacy by burning a worthless property in the black community? Who cares about protest? In 2012 there was a "Bring back our girls universal protest" for little girls who were violently kidnapped by Boko haram, did it work? Is there any instance where a protest have ever worked? Didn't we learn from the Sharpeville Massacre? Marikina and many events where black men get killed and arrested for protesting for their right to social respect? We need innovative means to be implemented in the pursuit to our Black glory. With that being said, we need to understand that the warfare have now regenerated to psychological and biological warfares. We need to own our information in order to win this psychological warfare over our black community, black babies, black women and black babies. I encourage you to bear in mind that there are people in control of information, education and the logical cosmological development of Africa today; and it is for a direct motive. If information can be controlled, then knowledge can be controlled; history can be regulated, science can be measured, and politics too can be manipulated by those who control the economy. Africa is a home to every race in the world as Credo Mutwa has said it enigmatically that "Africans are a Golden link that connects humanity together". History tells that, there are Europeans, who are of African descent in Ancient history (Greeks); we have Asians who are interconnected to Ancient African history and have their spiritual echo systems rooted in African civilisation. It's not necessarily "physical pigmentation" that comprises a race of people as Steve Biko would argue but their origin and genetic inheritance. Hence, leaders like Robert Sobukwe, a man who received much hostility from the "colonial Whiteman" because of his extraordinary reasoning ability despite the "control Mind weapons" presented to black people has indicated that we only have one race on the surface of the planet, and that is the human race, which reveals that he never hated no "Whiteman" but he only undermined White Supremacy and hatred. I should therefore, elucidate that, as a Blackman, during colonialism, slavery and entrapment, they have indoctrinated you, taken your history from you, your self-worth, your dignity, and have conditioned you to depend upon other races, and they taught you to hate your own kind hence you kill, rape and self-destruct your

own self. So all that has formed a new beast in the inside of you –
And that's what is today known as the 'Blackman" (Dehumanized
African). Let me clarify something to you; the words 'Black', 'Niger',
'Kaffir' and 'non-white' were designed for you to agree to the
complex of inferiority. And the word "White" was designed for the
Whiteman to benefit from the complex of Supremacy. Colonialism
and slavery were both an arrangement of dehumanization for the
Blackman who is the number 1 Public enemy in the whole world,
and in order to convince you that you are a barbarian who has
been liberated by the Whiteman's expansionism and imperialism.
There is no way on earth that a race of people can be classified in
colour and not through their continental inheritance; because those
who are classified "Blacks" are not even black. There is brown,
light brown, fair skin, light skin and dark; so why must they be
limited to some colour meant to discredit and pervert their race?
Asians identify themselves Asian not Pink or maroon, and those
who identify as "White" are not even white; some are red, some
light skin, some Pink etc., so why must they be limited to one
colour meant to promote Supremacy over other races? Black People
of African descent must be classified African, people of European
descent must be classified European, people of Australian descent
must be classified Australian, and People of Asian descent must be
classified Asian etc. Racism on its own is the art and science of
alienating other races in the pursuit to promote your own; and that
is inhumanity.

A "Blackman's" condition today is worse than ever before, more than it was back in colonialism and slavery. Other races have developed their homelands throughout the 400 years of colonization and slavery; even if they did so through the exploitation of other races. Africa today is portrayed as a home of poor people who cannot help themselves, a gang waiting for some International miracles through the International Aid, the World Bank and the International Monetary Fund which are "control-freak Organizations" who survives only in bloodsucking and "debt imperialism." We have been crippled psychologically, economically, ideologically and otherwise; so now is the time to usher in the reparations of our own BLACK mass and we shall recover, we shall win, we shall be competent again, we shall be scientific prodigies again and we shall bounce back to reality. It may seem impossible but I guarantee you that everything I have said is possible; but only if we can develop high consciousness and reason, be united enough to protect our own SELF from universal degradation, humiliation and the castration we are going through today. Be united enough to credit, uplift and pride ourselves in our own kind because there is nothing wrong with being proud of your own race. There is nothing wrong with being conscious of your own kind, there is nothing wrong with your history and likeness, there is nothing wrong with being African as much as there is nothing wrong with being European, Asian, American, Australian etc. It makes sense that many Africans regard Black Consciousness and Black Nationalist thinking as a teaching of the past and a "backward uncivilized political madness" because they are dehumanized and they know nothing rather than what the colonial and slave crackers have fed to them – indoctrination. And any Black person who believes that standing up against Black psychological Homicide is racism, is ipsa facto culturally homeless. First, Black consciousness is not a political or a drastic teaching in any way; Just like Steve Biko would have said: "It's a mental attitude and way of life". It is the redemption of the Knowledge of SELF, a reflection of truth within SELF after the white detraction of the black truth for a long time and the rejection of European definitions of BLACK, it is about accepting your likeness as a race and not depend on western portrayals of your history that identifies you as a barbarian in the past and as a substandard savage walking barefooted. This is about enchanting pride in SELF and developing a million degrees of consciousness that will re-uplift your race from the universal ignominy we are going through.

Can BLACK SELF-KNOWLEDGE help reinvent a new and positive impression of Africa - an Africa truly independent? Yes, it helps, and let me show you how. You must understand that your black SELF have been taught to think less about yourself, they have proselytized you to believe that you are neither industrious nor useful enough, and that you have made no progress to human civilization before western colonization, interventionalism and the slave trade. They suggest that before they came you were singing and dancing with monkeys, barefoot, and living in "grass-house" shelter and your economy was in the form of cattle and livestock, they tell you that regardless of the fact that Africa is rich in natural resources; African mineral resources were discovered by some earliest European imperialists. You have been fed with wrong information - that you invented nothing.

So with these forms of fallacies and indoctrinations, when you study the condition of contempt that the Black Nation faces today you then feel like your people are nothing and they will do nothing in the shallow of the universe without the Whiteman. This then propels you to worship Europeans, Americans, Asians, and Australians because you feel they are loftier and invented these many things and you only provide labor and that's it!

But let me remind you that BLACK SELF-KNOWLEDGE will help rewrite all these wrongs by teaching you the real truth of who you really are in order to re-activate your naturally given super power - Melanin. You have introduced civilization to mankind during the Dark Age/Ice Age, you invented Mathematics, Architecture, Engineering, Medicine, Mining of Minerals, Metallurgy, Astrology, Fishing, Metal chisels, saws, copper, glue, Bronze weapons, art, Gold refinery, Coins, steel fabrics, Jewellery, Clothing, Science, Writing systems, Letters/alphabets etc. You are not substandard as portrayed and misrepresented by western media; but colonialism have crippled you so effectively that you do not even recognize who you are, and despite all that, they didn't destroy you completely and you have every right to wake-up from that slave-sleep and participate in universal relations as an equal.

Black Consciousness awakens you from that "Slave-sleep" because when we have to say that Africa may be independent once again and re-develop its own continent and resume the universal race in development; you can understand that topic and actually play a major role in the reparations of the BLACKMAN and his Kaffired self. Many WHITE SUPREMACISTS don't want you to be SELF-PRESERVING because they understand that their interests will be uneased if you wake up from indoctrination and dehumanisation as the black society emanating from a distraughtly present influenced by the brutal past; hence, the teachings of Black Nationalism are regarded as robust, racist and uncivilized. How can taking pride in one's race be uncivilized? How can the teaching of one's history be uncivilized? How can the love of SELF be uncivilized? Maybe, in that case, we must then ask what "Civilization" really means.

Does civilization mean that Africans must find comfort in being portrayed and misrepresented as barbarians who lived in trees and caves with monkeys long before colonization? Does it mean that Africans must accept a wrong fiction about their real no-fictitious history and teach such a fairy-tale to their children and generations to come? Does it mean that Africans must remain dependent on Western Modern Day slavery? Does it mean that Africans must submit to "White Supremacy" by promoting the "Black inferiority?" Well, I don't understand what is being meant by "Black Consciousness" as an uncivilized teaching; but whatever that is – It plays a major role in the 21st century's indoctrination of the BLACKMAN. The truth shall set the human strength of mind free, the truth may hurt the enemy but it shall set us all who believe in the equality of mankind free. SELF-LOVE is stronger than any other form of love; and since charity begins at home, I urge you to love, respect, protect, honor and take pride in SELF, because it is the beginning of all wisdom. When the WHITEMAN came into Africa (Except for Ethiopia where many African countries descends from) at first they were coming in as trade partners and students of the African Science in countries like Zaire (Congo – Where many Bantu people mainly in Southern Africa today comes from.), Egypt (Which was formerly occupied by the "Bantu" people known as the "Black Pharaohs before Arabs occupied that land and where many European religious scholars were equipped), Mali (Where some of the Bantu people from some central African countries come from), they were here to learn and do business. But when the western felon realized that there were emerging countries in Africa in which those countries were underdeveloped and mainly unprotected, they then developed forms of capitalism and ferocious schemes and went back to craft weapons on their return to Europe. Africa may have been the earliest developed continent; but one thing they never put into mind was: The creation of weapons to defend themselves during times of catastrophe because this was a peaceful continent. So, the WHITEMAN then figured and studied the basics of blacks in those new emerging countries; like Ivory Coast, Ghana, Nigeria and mainly Southern African countries like South Africa, Zimbabwe, Zambia etc. Those basics were livestock,

Land, Women, minerals, Religion and love. So they came down and rendered themselves as religious cronies (Although there is a belief system that they introduced Jesus to Africans for which is a red lie; they used religion because Africans were a religious people) then after they realized that they are receiving attention in shaping the religious status quo of those new emerging African countries, they then went back to the then developed African countries like Egypt, Ethiopia, Zaire and Mali to learn and steal more knowledge and then came back to apply it as best as they could. So when those African countries realized that the Europeans were as good priests as their brothers in North-East Africa, they then welcomed them and gave them love (Second basic won). After religion and love were earned; those WHITES wanted to come with means to take over the land, livestock and minerals in order to fully break the BLACKMAN completely. But there was no peaceful way to achieve that objective.

So, out of desperation, hate, scorn, deception, jealousy, infidelity, dishonor, and dis-appreciation they then forcefully and violently took over the land and livestock to further break the BLACKMAN completely and they destroyed/killed anyone who stood on their way to so doing; which then contributed to the earliest African genocide which took place in the 14th century. After taking over some portions of Africa forcefully, the Portuguese and French colonies then introduced the Slave-trade to sell African slaves to mainly Jewish clients in various countries all over the world.

So, as much as the WHITEMAN took away the BLACKMAN's important basics to life, it was obvious that after having been crippled to that degree, males couldn't therefore, take care or rather protect their wives from colonial victimizations; such as rape, slavery and genocide. So this means that the AFRICAN FEMALE had to suffer the violation of being raped in front of her husband, children, parents while the AFRICAN MALE witnesses and do nothing about it and were forced to obey their colonial masters, honor and respect them although their colonial masters abused their wives, kids or family in front of them. An African female then felt that there is no need to respect such a man who witnesses her pain and does nothing about it, and there began the earliest introductions of the "Black inferiority complex" and also the promotion of "White Supremacy.". And today, after over 400 years of slavery and colonialism, the African male and the African female do not get along fully because the process of indoctrination was so broad that it may even last for up to a thousand years as mentioned by Willie Lynch in 1712 on his letter of making a slave, which he wrote for the slave owners of Virginia in the USA. The BLACKMALE is convinced that he is free from the White Supremacist chains; yet, he is still crippled economically, mentally, scientifically, psychologically and otherwise. But I should blame it on you BLACKMAN that your woman is back on your hands again yet you are the one who rapes her, you abuse her, you impregnates the BLACK WOMAN and then leave her with your beautiful babies for them to become single mothers while you continue to live free as if everything is okay; while you know well that deep within you have refused to be responsible. You do not protect your own women, you fight against them, you open up strip clubs and then recruit them to show-off their respectful bodies; you open up clubs and then recruit them to become prostitutes for them to please your clients – You have become so selfish that you are more attached to money in a manner that you forget the credibility of your African female.

You produce rap and house music videos and recruit them as Video Vixens; did you even forget what happened to Sarah Baartman? That part of you is called selfishness in the love of money; and you have sold out your own race because of the love of money. How do you expect other races to take you seriously when you cannot protect your own women? So you think that other races will respect them on your behalf? Some of you get married today and then divorce the following day; what kind of morality is in that? Why do you marry a person if you do not know them completely? Well, to be specific, we must undo the damage executed by colonial victimization because today the struggle we are fighting is in the mind, since they took it away from you. Well, there is also nothing glorious with most African females. Most of you BLACK WOMEN have thrown away your dignity; how do you become a prostitute and expect the BLACK society to take you seriously? How do you become a stripper and expect society to take you seriously? How do you become a video vixen and expect society to take you seriously? I actually commend most women; those for whom still see a reason to live despite their male counterparts' having impregnated them and left them as single mothers. That part of you shows resilience and productivity. But I don't expect you to use that against the BLACK MALE, because that was Willie Lynch's goal; to break the BLACKMAN so his African female can then looks at him as weak and ineffective. Unfortunately, that is happening today – Don't fall for that trick!

Dear Black Woman: Try to be independent, I know it's not easy; but if you depend on a man, you are likely to become his slave. Being independent and self-respecting is your sole dignity! If you have no self-respect and independence; you have no dignity! Sisters, you have every right to stand for women's rights (Feminism); but then, fighting for women's rights doesn't mean that a group of women must fight against the entire male image as if it is an image of the devil; those rights must be based on behavior and other things not against gender. Because usually, there are females who portray themselves as feminist but are organized with the mere purpose of hating the male image as a whole.

With that behavior then, the African image deteriorates every single day because both Males and Females must sit down together and undo all the injustices of the past by joining hands and standing together in restoring the entire African race pride instead of fighting against one another. Women must understand that they have all the ability to help the African male shackle the rise of his condition because they understand the genetic dialectics of creation and have all in their power to contribute to raising young and conscious children who knows exactly who they are and what world they live in so they can grow up and play a major role in moral commiseration. How is it possible that you don't control your own mind? As much as we all know that colonialism and slavery existed for so long, how is it possible that indoctrination is distributed to unborn African babies in post-colonialism? I thought indoctrination and mass incarceration took great shape during colonialism and not now; but then, just like Willie Lynch said "hate is stronger than love," it so clear that the colonial and slave masters introduced a system designed to redistribute from generation to generation even when African children are not yet born because they hated you so much they did all in their might to destroy you, and today you are set for psychological race extermination. So when you are born you find a system of indoctrination - waiting for you and you become a part of it from day one.

And when you grow up you look at the BLACK society from inferior lenses and then becomes ignorant to the knowledge of SELF, much that you don't even care about what happens to anyone except for you, your mother, your wife/husband and family. Race on its own is a family; so you must protect, care for, defend, fight for, honor, pride yourself in it because it shapes your image as a collective human brand. Martin Luther King Jr. said that "A Ghetto is a domestic colony" And it makes sense that Africans were segregated to rural and township neighborhoods where their economics are remotely controlled - And don't you think it's the third part of Willie Lynch's vision?

To position slaves in a manner that if those methods are effected properly they can last for up to a thousand years? And today, after colonialism, you are still staying in rural and township neighborhoods where there are no industries and strategic economic divisions, and the only thing left out for you is to move out to the preceding imperialist's neighborhood they prepared knowingly that when you get fed up of the underdevelopment of your neighborhood you will come there and play by their rules, pay large amounts of rent and you don't even qualify for a housing subsidy without the help of banks that also belongs to them. Whereby you are given a 20-year repayment plan knowingly that you cannot financially sustain to that period, and that time when you go under a financial drought they take you out of their neighborhood without compensation and you get back to where you came from – rural and township neighborhood because that's the place they designed for you. I don't blame you for moving out from a poor neighborhood because that's where the system of colonialism placed you and you will never be productive as an individual living in a crippled neighborhood; and since the government has turn a blind eye to the reparations of the African race the only way we can deal with the process of reparations is by acknowledging there is a problem in our neighborhoods and we must get rid of that problem which have crippled us for so long. We can repair ourselves by industrializing rural and township neighborhoods – by building clothing industries, Agriculture, production industries, Malls, Museums, Science factories, Technological industries etc. (And we will be creating enough jobs for our people in those neighborhoods so there won't be any need to move out and play part in Urbanization because we would have urbanized our communities.) And we can BEGIN the reparation conversion from smaller things such as spending our monies in our communities. Dr. Claude Anderson teaches the practising of group economics for which is the same thing that Malcolm x taught, the same thing that Marcus Garvey taught, the same thing that Martin Luther KingJr. also taught in his later days. He says that the 'Black race" must learn to open their businesses and control them - "Asian money bounces 12 to 13 times in their communities before it goes to other communities, Jewish money bounces 18 times, White money bounces 14 to 15 times and Black money doesn't bounce at all. As soon they get paid they go straight to other communities and spend it. And well that's true, we don't practice group economics. Today you feel some credibility for spending your money at Pick n' Pay more than when you spend it in a supermarket in the community where you are from. How are those mini supermarkets going to grow into mega Supermarkets when you do not support them? Are there people from other races coming and supporting businesses in your neighborhood? Pakistanis and Indians have now opened many businesses in your neighborhood and you have been their loyal clients for long; hence, their businesses grow every single day. You can be loyal to them for long but they clarify it to you that you are not important; and that your money is what they toured into your mini-community for. Hence when you are short with 0.1 % of what you are purchasing they will never give it to you because you have no space in their world. When you try to practice the same method by going into their neighborhoods and open the very same nature of businesses they open in your neighborhoods they will never buy from you, not because they hate or rather discriminate you but because they are conscious enough to protect their own SELF as a collective brand and that's intelligence – That's what you must practice as well. We must practice group economics, we have to practice group economics, we can practice group economics – And we must practice group economics. If needs it be, let's boycott supporting all foreign businesses which play no part in social responsibility programs such as sponsoring activities and donating to charities etc. from restaurants to clothing businesses like McDonalds, Wimpy, Spur, Mugg&bean, Cappello, Woolworths, Shoprite, Edgars, Spitz, Truworths, Debonairs Pizza, Levi's, Daniel Hecter, Jonathan D, Louis Vitom, Red Square, Lacostè, Clicks, Vodacom, Pakistani/Chinese/Indian mini markets, Pick n' Pay, Checkers etc. And support our own businesses so they can grow and become like those businesses I mentioned that we take much pride in supporting. Why do you take a Pick N Pay plastic instead of buying from a Black Tuck Shop or a Markhams plastic when you know they won't be buying from Markhams? Is this how much dominant white centralized business have done for you that you are ashamed of your own black businesses? Have you ever seen any Indian person buying from the INDIAN shop that you buy from? Or any WHITE person BUYING FROM THE WHITE RESTAURANT that you BUY FROM? (KFC, CHICKEN LICKEN, SPITS etc) if not we need to start asking ourselves QUESTIONS. First of all; who is the number one Public enemy? YOU ARE. So if someone cook you SOMETHING TO eat but they don't eat the SAME FOOD THEMSELVES, and one who don't like you at all, will you EAT the same food with an OPEN heart? If so please openly allow me to confirm that you are a fully DEHUMANIZED GROUP and you need to swallow differences and come together, unite and organize!

We need to start supporting businesses which actually cares about us as a race and which understands the process of reparations that we are going through rather than some capitalistic felons who pay no regard to our struggles whatsoever. All these businesses have all in their power to support the process of reparations that Africans as a race are going through; only if they can participate fully in social responsibility programs especially to underdeveloped neighborhoods like rural and townships. But if they don't care at all then we must stop running madly by going to support such kind of businesses because they are equally responsible for the destruction of the African image as much as the preceding colonial and slave masters do. We have little time to play hide and seek with our race because we have been disrespected for a long time, and maybe it's now time to claim our dignity back.

Today, after the total destruction of our race as a people we are the most scrawny in the planet; proof is we hate each other because that's what we have been taught during slavery and colonialism; we kill each other (Black on Black violence) while other races protect their own SELF and join hands to build societies they can be proud of. We are the only race that gang up against each other and that's what use to happen back in colonialism; your colonial master would hire you to kill your own brother and then praise you for being smart and you would then rejoice and celebrate that madness because back then it was understandable – You didn't have a choice. Because back then if you didn't do what you were told to do you would then be killed by that colonial master. We discriminate against each other based on the language/tribe one belongs to; they divided you in order to rule you effectively, and today that system of Divide-and-rule is in place and alive. We spy on each other, hence it was easy to destroy the life of Malcolm X, and hence it was easy to get rid of Martin Luther King Jr. Hence it was easy to get rid of Steve Biko; hence it was easy to get rid of Patrice Lumumba, Thomas Sankara, and Chris Hani etc. We cannot stand each other because we have been designed that way throughout imperialism. They have studied you and they know you better than you know yourselves; because they owned you. Did you know that Black people pay more interest than WHITES from BANKS on car loans, House loans, PERSONAL LOANS etc? and pay more premiums on Insurance, life and funeral policies than RICH white people? So their resonance is that you are a greater risk by DEFAULT and hey that's your newly found FREEDOM, JUSTICE & EQUALITY. They make it difficult for you to earn a decent LIVING because by DEFAULT they expect you to be a subservient being! I therefore urge you to stand up together. There is no ZULU, no TSONGA, no SWATI, no Venda, no Xhosa, Ndebele, Tswana, Sotho or Pedi. You all are "Black people/Africans" and should stand up and swallow your tribalist psychological infernos. Love, care and Protect your own KIND! We don't look up on each other, we still judge each other based on class and material accumulations instead of bending together in this era of decolonization; We hurt each other up, we are jealous of one another much that we even kill each other because of jealousy, hatred and scorn. We are more concerned in developing ourselves as individuals instead of developing ourselves as a race like Europeans do, like Americans do, like Asians do and like everyone else does. We don't believe in ourselves much that we let other countries dictate what kind of educational system is suitable for us, what kind of an economic system suit us and also the political system that suits us and yet we expect to be treated as an equal player in international trade and economic relationships. Young African females must stop listening to interferences because "you" women listen to a lot of unnecessary trash— You are told that your hair is not good enough and you go ahead and buy fake hair in order to fit in; you are told that your eyelashes are not good enough and you go ahead to buy fake eyelashes in order to fit in; you are told that your skin is not light enough and you go ahead to buy painting cream in order to fit in; you are told that your nails are not good enough and you go ahead and buy fake nails in order to fit in, you are told that your lips are not sexier enough and you go ahead and buy lipstick in order to fit in; you are told that your breasts are not good enough and you go ahead and buy push-up bras in order to fit in, you are told that your height is not good enough and you go ahead and buy High Heel Shoes" (shoes primarily designed for modellers and strippers) in order to fit in and today you are told that your booty is not good enough and you still go ahead and put a "Fake booty" in order to fit in. So most of your struggles as women are vested in trying to fit into what the other side says about you. There is no African company that produces fake hair, there is no African company that produces fake eyelashes, there is no African company that produces fake nails etc. Those are produced by other races with you in mind. Do Brazilian women pride themselves in buying "African hair?" So why do you pride yourself in putting an original Brazilian hair and brag about it? Is it because it is expensive or you think Brazilian hair is better than African hair? Well, I don't know what your answer to that is but I think you have a very great mind problem. I encourage you to feel proud in who you are and be confident about it – If you have short hair take care of it; If you have coarse hair take care of it, if you have long hair take care of it, if you are dark embrace yourself that way, if you are light do the same; my point is, whatever you have as part of your appearance package try to find peace in it instead of trying to become something you are not just because you want to fit in.

How do you expect other races to take you serious with that behavior? And how do you expect your own male to respect you when you don't respect what God gave you? I do not condemn you or rather to promote anything negative; I'm trying to bring into awareness the weight of your behavior as a race. As for the Blackman, so you call yourself a blesser for abusing desperate and young Black women? If you were a blesser you would create jobs for them and demand nothing in return! This woman is your strength, you need to start respecting and protecting her, she is the mother of civilisation and have gone through hell for centuries and it's your time to show up and stand along your black woman.

Today, many African countries think that they are independent when none controls their own economy, maybe with the exclusion of Zimbabwe (for now). Whether you like it or not, many African countries are controlled by the Foreign elitist corporate system incorporated within the free market economic system (Capitalism) which many African governments are practicing while history proves that Capitalism cannot survive without blood sucking. So it is obvious that if you do not control your economy, then modern day imperialism/colonialism/slavery is in great existence and very much alive. I know most of you need some proof on this sensitive topic; but let's use common sense to measure this – Let me say there is a household of two parents (Mother and father) and three children; Firstborn, second born and last born. Even if in reality, the parents in that household are the ones responsible for setting up rules that will govern any member of that household but they do not have the financial capacity to take care of that household. If the last born is the one who is paying all the bills and groceries in that house, his words will be the ones that matters than any other person in that house despite he being the youngest person in that family; If he says "today we are eating chicken" everybody will eat chicken, If he says "he is going to buy new furniture and the old one must be donated to charity" the entire family will stand by his words and not the other way round because if they go against him he will withdraw his contribution.

So you need to understand that money has been given the power to control everything in the society starting with the regulation of government and the political elite. And if indeed those who run the economy, therefore, controls the 1. Political elite (In order to ensure that he influences the public through propaganda and diplomatic policies) then they control the 2. Government (And dictate a system that will benefit them alongside the political elite and not the people) then they control the 3. Educational system (educate the people's outlooks on what they want you to know and to measure up your level of intellectual capacity so that they can keep you ignorant to the knowledge of yourself) then the 4. Media system (To regulate the kind of content that goes into your system and also to ridicule any form of radicalism and organized attempts to alter in social revolution and to alter unity and active social cohesiveness so that their stay in power cannot be troubled) then the 5. Means of production (In order to maintain their control of the state without any trouble) that means they also control the entire public, and you become a victim of the federal government's inability to change your condition that has been created by the very same systems for 400 years and yet you cannot bend together and repair yourselves while it is clear that the government, the political and the economic elite are not willing to change your condition.

Basically, I don't think that we need the government in order to begin the process of reparations. Asians were colonized too but look at what they have done in post-colonialism as compared to us. The system of divide-and-rule is in progress in many African countries, we are facing a tribal hatred in Rwanda, Burundi, Zimbabwe, South Africa, Congo and many African countries in post-colonialism because we haven't taken it upon ourselves to repair our minds and the societies we live in. But we have a problem - a very great problem. Today we are vanity slaves, we are proud of the image that the evils of the world painted of us hence we are very ignorant to almost everything. We are ignorant to the true knowledge of ourselves while there are people busy dying for us to be conscious of the true knowledge of Africanism as opposed to some picture painted by International Media about Africa. If we are a poor race today it is because Europe and America have fought hard to make us this way and that's not a racist teaching. If we are a weaker continent today that is all because Europe and America weakened us and that's not a racist teaching. They ruled us, they turned us into commodity and today we are struggling to function without some form of psychological help/dependency.

"No living white person is responsible for slavery, but all living whites reap its benefit, just like all living blacks wear its scars" - Unknown

There is something I do not understand - All African countries which were colonized (Which means all the 53 African states, with the exclusion of Ethiopia because it was never colonized) are paying back a debt that was used to enslave them for 400 years to the world bank and the International Monetary Fund, a debt they didn't even use but was used by a slave system. Can't there be a new beginning without the intrusion of the World Bank? If there is no such reality then there is no African country that can claim their independence at this point — We are all slaves and cowardice to confront this occult behavior that is fed to us by the West and America; this must come to an end!

There is no international treaty, not even the United Nations have advocated for the reparations of all Africans who are victims of slavery and colonialism and are living everywhere all over the world with a sense of persecuted thinking, and also victimized and destroyed communities; so, the bill acquired through the exploitation of an African child is today paid by the victims.

So does that mean that the "bloodsucking Capitalism" is better than human life and respect? Well, nothing is free about Africa and Africans, we are still to undergo that process of emancipation and reparations and I hope there can't be a Third World War for Africans to get an internationally acclaimed respect and independence. Africans must be able to recognize that the world is against them and that means we have to create a world of our own, a world that will respect our image as a race, a world that will honor the image of Africanism, and the world that will think like humans not like programmed computers. Malcolm X said that "If you live in a poor neighborhood, you are living in an area whereby you have poor schools, when you have poor schools you get poor teachers, and when you have poor teachers you will get a poor education, and with poor education you can only work in a poor paying job, and with a poor paying job you will again live in a poor neighborhood."

Well, that statement is still relevant today and was cited in the 60's (Approximately over 50 years ago). How possible is it that those who value Africanism are killed and nothing happens after their death? – No change of behavior in Africans and no defense from the African Union because something is wrong with that Organization. Slavery was never an accident, it was planned and it has been effectively structured. I would like to quote a letter by Willie Lynch titled "The Making of a Slave" (To the Colony of Virginia on December 25, 1712) it reads:

Gentlemen, I greet you here on the banks of the James River in the year of our Lord one thousand seven hundred and twelve. First, I shall thank you, the gentlemen of the Colony of Virginia for bringing me here. I am here to help you solve some of your problems with slaves. Your invitation reached me on my

modest plantation in the West Indies were I have experiment-
ed with some of the newest and still the oldest methods for
control of slaves. Ancient Rome would envy us if my program
is implemented. As our boat sailed south on the James River,
named for our Illustrious King, whose version of the Bible we
cherish, I saw enough to know your problem is not unique.
While Rome used cords of wood as crosses for standing human
bodies along its old highways in great numbers, you are here
using the tree and rope on occasion. I caught the whiff of a
dead slave hanging from a tree a couple of miles back. You are
not only losing valuable stocks by hangings, you are having up-
risings, slaves are running away, your crops are sometimes left
in the fields too long for maximum profit, you suffer occasion-
al fires, your animals are killed. Gentlemen, you know what
problems are; I do not need to elaborate. I am not here to enu-
merate your problems; however, I am here to introduce you to
a method of solving them. In my bag here, *I have a foolproof
method for controlling your Black slaves.* I guarantee every one
of you that if it is installed correctly, *it will control the slaves for
at least 300 years.* My method is simple. Any member of your
family or your overseer can use it. *I have outlined a number
of DIFFERENCES among the slaves, and I take these differences and make them bigger. I use FEAR, DISTRUST, and ENVY
for control purposes.* These methods have worked on my modest plantation in the West Indies and it will work throughout

the South. Take this simple little list of differences, and think about them. On the top of my list is *"AGE"but it is there only because it starts with an "A": the second is "COLOR' or SHADE, there is INTELLEGENCE, SIZE, SEX, SIZE PLANTATIONS, STATUS ON PLATATION, ATTITUDE OF OWNERS, WHETHER THE SLAVES LIVE IN THE VALLEY, ON THE HILL, EAST, WEST, NORTH, SOUTH, HAVE FINE HAIR, COARSE HAIR, OR IS TALL OR SHORT.* Now that you have a list of differences, *I shall give you an outline of action –but before that, I shall assure you that DISTRUST is stronger than TRUST, and ENVY is stronger than ADULATION, RESPECT, OR ADMIRATION.* The Black salve after receiving this indoctrination shall carry on and will become self refuelling and self generation for hundreds of years, maybe thousands. Don't forget, you must pitch the OLD BLACK MALE vs. the YOUNG BLACK MALE and the YOUNG BLACK MALE against the OLD BLACK MALE. You must use the Dark Skin Slaves vs. the Light Skin Slaves and the Light Skin Slaves vs. the Dark Skin Slaves. You must use the Female vs. the Male, and the Male vs. the Female. You must also have your white servants and overseers Distrust all Blacks, but it is necessary your slaves trust and depend on us. The must love, respect, and trust only us. Gentlemen, these kits are the keys to control. Use them. Have your wives and children use them, never miss an opportunity. If used intensively for one year, the slaves themselves will remain perpetually distrustful. Thank you, gentlemen."

So can you say that Willie Lynch's letter was lunacy given the pre-intended "mind control scheme"? Don't you think that Willie Lynch is proud of his methods in his grave today?

What the WHITEMAN has done preeminently was to teach you to hate yourself, to hate one another, to kill each other, to be divided so they can conquer you. And today you ask yourself where tribalism really comes from. Tribalism is part of Willie Lynch and the Whiteman's syndrome. In fact, tribalism should be renamed to "Willie Lynch's syndrome". Tribalism is a mental docile, where members of the same group discriminate each other based on the different tribes they come from, at least that's my understanding of the concept. So if you are from a Zulu tribe, you discriminate one from the Tswana tribe, and one from the Tswana tribe discriminate one from the Swahili tribe etc. and this is regardless of whether or not, these men come from the same race. Through Willie Lynch's methods, you have been qualified to perfect tribalism amongst yourselves, to believe that your tribe is better than your own brother and sister's tribe. But, well, if you think that way then you are no different to your preceding racist imperialist who call you monkeys.

However, in all of this, it is not rational to blame the mis-educations, mental incarcerations and indoctrinations inflicted upon our people without providing solutions towards such startling problems; but leaders, overseers, intellectuals and motivational speakers all have a responsibility to provide solutions to all the problems they may delineate in their exposition since theory without practice is just a song without tune. We all know the truth, we all have capacity, we all have experiences that can be of best benefit to those around us, we all can change this animal (Willie Lynch's Syndrome); but the congestion we have is unwillingness, foolishness and also blinded by colonial conventionalism. Willie Lynch's syndrome has been a well-practiced metaphysical act in almost every diversified African community just after colonialism and was well planted in the roots of Alkabulan. But the divisional mathematics, science and the extremism of intermediate destructive psychology have existed, just after the colonial syndrome was spread all over Africa. And In order to master the science of Willie Lynch's tactics, in order for us to come up with a vigorous solution to this enemy of morality we must discuss its development and mound within our community in order to plant realization and awareness; hence, I quoted Willie Lynch's letter for you to have a clue of what philosophical subscription the Colonial crackers bows down to.

And despite the fact that you have been colonized for long, look at what you have done to yourself. You spend your weekends and your financial savings in Clubs and Taverns. Every Black Community has a set of clubs and taverns and those are filled up by people who should be repossessing their image as humans after having been dehumanized, oppressed, castrated, taught to dishonor, discredit, and disregard their own kind and to perceive themselves as commodity to white capital. And After being economically exterminated you then save money not to invest or buy important stuff such as production machinery in order to produce products of our own and feed our people, Farms in order to do agriculture, Malls in order to empower our own Black businesses; but instead invest money to buy alcohol - get drunk and continue to be a slave, and then the following day, after having spent all the money you have worked hard for in beer and prostitutes you then go ahead and beg the system of exploitation to empower you with a job. In other words, you go back to other races who have shown no regard or respect for you and beg them to give you a job so you can become their faithful slave for eternity. Our people can work for another race for more than 15 years and still fail to see anything wrong with that – We are vanity slaves! The majority of people in Africa are Africans, and Africans are more than a billion in counting. Imagine how many brains and resources can be put together to redevelop an African image if those people were united, supporting their own businesses, joining resources and working together towards progress. We can never fail to uplift ourselves but we have proven to the world that we are proud graduates of Willie Lynch's methods and we cannot even resist a simple thing such as self-hate. We hate each other that we discriminate ourselves based on tribal differences, we kill each other, we rape our women, we kidnap our own babies, we compete against each other, and we spy against one another. We are a rotten bunch of people who pay no attention to self-love. We cannot even produce our own car but we are living in the 21st century although we introduced civilization to the world. We produce no phones but we claim to be free and independent, we produce no computers but we are so addicted to technology than any other race. We don't understand the production processes of the internet and telephone cables and one day they may cut those things down if they realize that you are becoming stronger as a race in order to disconnect your communication methods. You must learn to mobilize your own people without Europeanized capitalism in the process and put a stop to the suffering of the Black race as a result of the deliberate human exploitation by the colonial Cracker.

You must learn to establish/create your own communication technologies or channels – The internet, computers, Telephone networks, email systems, electrical systems, Nuclear systems, and military systems too because you never know what will happen next in a society; so better be safe than anything else that is unknown. Many rich countries continue targeting the weaker ones in order to drink the blood of the poor by feeding the crown of the rich and you are a number one target in that quandary because you are the number one weak continent on the planet; and again, this is not hate but the truth. There is no other race begging us to give them jobs because they know that we produce nothing, the only thing we do today is labor. Therefore they have every right to disrespect us if we give them such an impression that they are the ones capable of producing everything because that's what they claim to be. I do not believe that there is any one man from any race who can claim to be better than me because I know my Ancient majestic image as opposed to an image that colonialists have created of Africans.

Self hate is contagious, and in my upbringing I used to say: "I wish I was born WHITE" because of their privilege, but that was long before I was redeemed in the name of self-determination, Self-knowledge and re-education from the shackles of Mis-education, Mind Control, Indoctrination and dehumanization. And don't act as if you were innocent either because you know what I'm talking about. It's hard for the Blackman out there and no man on 360 degrees of planet earth can aspire to be White unless he is ready to suck blood! I say so because History doesn't lie; it's only White People who have sucked the Blood of human life all over the world. Adolph Hitler was a Whiteman and he killed more than 11 million people, John Cecil Rhodes Was a Whiteman and he killed more than 16 million Black people and there are many instances of white genocides here in Africa and if I was to focus on the topic it would take the whole book. And although Whites have tried in all means to racially profile us as inferior, their White Self is White or pink because when the black man was still great here in Africa and had succeeded in running them across the Mediterranean into South Europe, they had to hide themselves in caves where there was very little light and air. So therefore, their PINKNESS or WHITENESS is nothing SUPERIOR but just a dire proof that they came from CAVES and not us!

The great Marcus Garvey advised: "'If others laugh at you, return the laughter to them; if they mimic you, return the compliment with equal force. They have no more right to dishonor, disrespect and disregard your feeling and manhood than you have in dealing with them. Honor them when they honor you; disrespect and disregard them when they vilely treat you. Their arrogance is but skin deep and an assumption that has no foundation in morals or in law. They have sprung from the same family tree of obscurity as we have; their history is as rude in its primitiveness as ours; their ancestors ran wild and naked, lived in caves and in the branches of trees, like monkeys, as ours; they made human sacrifices, ate the flesh of their own dead and the raw meat of the wild beast for centuries even as they accuse us of doing; their cannibalism was more prolonged than ours; when we were embracing the arts and sciences on the banks of the Nile their ancestors were still drinking human blood and eating out of the skulls of their conquered dead; when our civilization had reached the noonday of progress they were still running naked and sleeping in holes and caves with rats, bats and other insects and animals."

So it is then relevant for black people to speak life to each other for after 400 years of being portrayed as substandard humans they then carry with them, the inferiority complex making it difficult for their space to develop the positive attitude in our black babies. Sharing these kind of information may be perceived racist in nature, but a people whose dignity have been taken away from them, whose history have been taken away from them, whose minds have been taken away from them, whose science, knowledge, wisdom have been taken away from them, whose knowledge of self have been taken away from them requires a great rude awakening in order to recover and again meet the psychological demands of racial development. I say so, because whilst we believe that White Racism is in the past – the television, newspapers, radio etc. tells a different story. The Whiteman have oppressed, dehumanised and killed black people for over 380 years and today they make movies and benefit from your pain and shaming. Both Sarafina (produced in 1991) and Shaka Zulu (Produced in 1986) were produced by Hollywood – an American Production company, so how truthful can those dark stories be? They commercialise your humiliation and not even pay reparations, and many, would agree with me that Desmond Tutu's Truth and reconciliation Commission was an insult to Black people since they have failed to pay reparations except only for 17000 families out of millions of the Black Holocaust victims as much as Nelson Mandela, equally so, didn't do a thing for Black people rather than being a masquerade for White Liberalism.

For as long as the Black Nation allows itself to be oppressed continuously, we will have dysfunctional families, parents and dysfunctional babies because oppression requires that the victim be dysfunctional. And please stop buying your babies White Dolls, you are programming them. Black babies don't need no white dolls as much as White babies need no Black dolls, we need no Cinderella fiction, you need no white anything because your black self is sufficient evidence that God created man in his own image because you are GOD'S and until your Black self stop buying white dolls you are not fit to be identified human in 360 degrees of planet earth. You need to love your beautiful black self until your white friends hate you for loving yourself. And as for skin bleaching, I'm a little uncomfortable in dealing with this subject matter as I am trying by all means to avoid controversy. The likes of Khanyi Mbau have bleached their skin and are proud of the post-effects, but here is the thing; I want you to know that black people have White People skin layers in them. That's why you can bleach your skin and they cannot darken their skin, so how can you be inferior to a group which have only one skin layer? They don't have our dark superiority so they are not superior. If you are to buy a car, the White colour is the cheapest because any other colour is expensive since they have white colour underneath so I advise you to stop bleaching your melanin, and I'm not being racist, I'm bringing up new conversations and I have no better way for doing so than a Hard talk!

Both Black and White BABIES are being systematically Mis-educated to HATE BLACKNESS everyday at school. It is then difficult to imagine what the FUTURE holds for the BLACK NATION if the current generation sit DOWN and DO NOTHING; hence, I wrote this book to ensure that at least in their quest for knowledge and information they will hopefully learn a thing or two about the argument surrounding Black's racial profiling. Racial classification has a great deal of scientific typological effect in human study and that's why it is necessary to study and understand what WHITE is expected to mean and what BLACK is also positioned to describe. Black people do not exist nor white people either although Africans have shown credence to this madness. Those are only racial destruction doctrines. Imagine, what will a black person or a white person look like? To me if there were black people on earth they would be baboons and if there were white people, they would be ghosts. In my life, I will only respect those who promote the ideology of Pan-African consciousness instead of promoting the concept "Black" as a reflection of our identity; and also, to promote the ideology of Pan African's call for action. It is precisely correct and psychologically proven that knowledge is power; and we all know that. Africans are the only people in the world who do not own their natural aspect of humanity, we are living as though we are living in the first round and there will be a second round, but trust me – we will only live once.

The word BLACK represents death, it is synonymous to Shame (And you are Shameful; no wonder you call yourselves Black) it is usually aligned with Negativity. So are you Black or AFRICAN? In South Africa, there is a familiar concept that refers to being dealt with in the society, known as blacklist; blacklist is not a forthcoming concept because once you are blacklisted then it's no discrepancy with being banned in society. So that is to show that Black is no good, and defining yourself a Black person in this age is full-time idiocy. Chinese people were smart, they call themselves as what origin entails and not with color, and actually, Asians align their identity with their continental motherland. And instead of Africa to align themselves Africans they'd rather call themselves the Blacks of this world (In other words, the useless of this world and you are indeed useless to this day). Words has power and I expect you to respect yourself and start to take yourself seriously so that the world can respect you - Love yourself, honor yourself, pride yourself of your own kind, and I promise; your mental freedom will be attained that way.

CHAPTER TWO

THE CONSPIRACY IN AFRICAN HISTORY

"Until a lion learns how to write, every story will
glorify the hunter"

-Anonymous

A HISTORY OF A PEOPLE is like the oxygen we need in order to breathe in and out. And as much as that's the case, it is true that the history of Africa has always been narrated by European imperialists who have been and still are obsessed about "White Supremacy" and "Black inferiority". So the question is, why is it so important for European historians to write the history of Africans when Africans could do that for themselves? Is there anything they are hiding to the world? Maybe there is – And that is the ancient civilisation of mankind which was developed in Africa. The Ancient pre-colonial history of Africa reveals the real truth about the earliest civilizations of humanity; but Western media have tried in their might to clatter that fact from the eyes of the world in order to portray Africa as a home of barbarism and slaves who have been civilized by European colonialism, they claim to have brought civilization to Africa and that Africa was a jungle with a group of Africans singing and dancing with monkeys and staying in caves eating each other (Cannibalism) while reality tells that our people have always been paramount and they have been travelling all over the world to trade with European and Asian countries and the Americans long before Europe sailed into America, long before colonialism and the Slave-trade because our people invented the navigation systems around 3000 B.C. Many Ancient African countries (Mali, Egypt, Ethiopia, Zaire, and Timbuktu) created different types of boats, from small vessels to large ships of 80 tons.

Africa's original name was Alkabulan (Land of the Blacks) and was renamed to Africa only after being defeated by Scipio Africanus who defeated Hannibal at the final battle of the second Punic War at Zama around the 2nd century. The history of Africa as taught in African schools in the 21st century is the one that the slave and colonial masters have narrated. The one that starts at the beginning of the scramble of Africa during European invasions and also the wrong narrative about how Africa was before they came and there is nowhere in those school textbooks do they say anything to do with ancient civilization because they knew that since they conceptualized the system of "Black inferiority complex" and "White Supremacy"- when African babies or adults realizes their greater contribution to civilization they will mature into seeing nothing inferior with the African image and also nothing superior with the European image as promoted by both the educational and the media systems. Africa was colonized during the era of vexing to find trade routes and trade partners and also exported a lot of its scholars known as the Moors (Blacks in Arabic) to go to Europe and teach science education, Mathematics, astrology, art, agriculture architecture and also formed part of different military systems in Europe from around the 7th century till the 14th century which then helped Europe to navigate towards the Dark age into trading with Africa as an equal player. Although western media refers to Moors - as the Medieval Muslim inhabitants of the Maghreb, Iberian Peninsula, Sicily and Malta. That is a conspiracy against the "Black race's influence of the world" because Europe has done in all her might to narrate African history for Africans to regulate and control the true colours of the African's race history. An Author and historian, Chancellor Williams, said that "the original Moors, like the original Egyptians, were Black Africans" and the same issue applies to Egypt. The media refers to Egypt as the place of "Light skinned Arabs" who occupies Egypt but ancient Egypt was occupied by blacks long before their slave invasion on the people of Mesopotamia, these Africans were called the "Black Pharaohs". Proof is in all the Ancient Egyptian paintings, paintings of Black Africans looks brownish to indicate who lived in Egypt in Ancient times - the only brown people on earth are people of African descent. The Greek historian Herodotus; described the Colchians of the Black Sea shores as

"Egyptians by race" and pointed out they had "black skins and kinky hair." Apollodorus, the Greek philosopher, described Egypt as "the country of the black-footed ones" and the Latin historian Ammianus Marcellinus said, "the men of Egypt are mostly brown or black with a skinny desiccated look." In his book 'Egypt', British scholar, Sir E.A. Wallis Budge says: "The prehistoric native of Egypt, both in the old and in the new Stone Ages, was African and there is every reason for saying that the earliest settlers came from the South." Our historical records disclose that approximately 5000 to 6000 years ago great civilisations in West and North Africa (Zaire, Mali, Angola, Egypt, and Ethiopia) created clocks to augment their calendars. With their associated officialdoms, formal religions, and other burgeoning societal activities, these cultures apparently found a need to organise their time more efficiently. These happened years before colonisation and European invasion set their foot on African soil but they never teach this at schools because if they do the truth will come out and the "African indoctrinated Class" will be awake and that will trouble the western felons who capitalise on the ignorance of many Africans all over the world. We also had many beautiful places in Africa while the world was still asleep, places like Timbuktu. For Africans, Timbuktu was as important as Rome, Athens, Jerusalem, and Mecca are too many other races/ cultures. In the thirteenth century, Timbuktu became the centre of a thriving trade in Africa. The trade routes brought great wealth to the city. By 1330, Timbuktu was part of the powerful Mali Empire headed by Mansa Musa whom was the richest man on the planet in the 13th Century. Accompanied by an enormous group of people, Mansa Musa apparently brought and gave away so much gold in Cairo, Egypt on his religious pilgrimage to Mecca that the value of it (Gold) fell and did not recover for many years after.

The Mali empire, little known beyond the western Sudan, now became legendary in the Islamic world and Europe and that attracted European capitalists to realize that Africa was naturally blessed with natural resources as compared to Europe which is the second smallest of the seven continents with only 2% earth surface which makes it difficult for their world to produce enormous natural resources as compared to Africa. The image of Mansa Musa bearing hunks of gold was placed on maps of the African continent, which controlled the lucrative gold-salt trade routes in the West African region. Two centuries later (Around the 15th century), Timbuktu reached the height of its power under the Songhai Empire, becoming a central place for learning. From the early part of the fourteenth century to the time of the Moroccan invasion in the late sixteenth century, the city of Timbuktu became an important place for religion and learning, with people travelling large distances to learn there, mainly from Europe. Great mosques, universities, schools, and libraries were built, some of which still stand today. Timbuktu's golden age ended in the late sixteenth century when a Moroccan army destroyed the Songhai Empire. Around 400 years ago, European ships traded along the West African coast, and the trade routes that made Timbuktu important were not used. Having lost the source of its wealth, Timbuktu declined and became known as a lost city branded that way by western media. As part of playing a part in the education of society, Africa invented Mathematics. The oldest known possibly mathematical object is the Lebombo bone, which was discovered in the Lebombo Mountains of Swaziland and dated to approximately 35,000 B.C. Many of the maths concepts learned in school today were also developed in Africa. Over 35,000 years ago, Ancient Egyptians scripted textbooks about maths that included division and multiplication of fractions and geometric formulas to calculate the area and volume of shapes.

The Ishango bone, found near the headwaters of the Nile River (north-eastern Congo), may be as much as 20,000 years old and consists of a series of tally marks carved in three columns running the length of the bone. Common interpretations are that the Ishango bone shows either the earliest known demonstration of sequences of prime numbers or a six-month lunar calendar. Also, Predynastic Egyptians of the 5th millennium BC pictorially represented geometric designs. "Numeral systems have been many and diverse, with the first known written numerals created by Egyptians in Middle Kingdom texts such as the Rhind Mathematical Papyrus. The earliest uses of mathematics were in trading, land measurement, painting and weaving patterns and recording time. More complex mathematics did not appear until around 3000 BC, when the Egyptians and Babylonians began using arithmetic, algebra and geometry for taxation and other financial calculations, for building and construction, and for astronomy". Even the notion that Europeans introduced Engineering and Architecture or buildings to barbaric Africans is a red lie and also a promotion of the "Black inferiority complex". The African empire of Egypt industrialized an enormous collection of diverse architectural and engineering structures along the Nile, among the largest and most famous of which is the Great Pyramid of Giza which is believed to be the first building in the world as compared to Europe's cave paintings (the most famous being the Cave of Lascaux complex in modern day France 20,000 BC) although Europe claims to have introduced buildings to Africans living in caves while history and reality tells that they are the ones who were living in caves – And this is not comparison to European history but I am making you aware of your colonial master's history since he also writes your history. Another famous building which was built alongside the great Pyramids of Giza is the Great Sphinx of Giza. Later, in the 12th century, there were hundreds of great cities in Zimbabwe and Mozambique made of massive stone complexes and huge castles like compounds. In the 13th century, the empire of Mali paraded extraordinary cities including Timbuktu with grand palaces, mosques and universities as already indicated. Most Ancient African countries (Zaire, Mali, Egypt, Ethiopia, Ghana etc.) discovered metallurgy and tools; these include steam engines, metal chisels and saws, copper and iron, tools and weapons, nails, glue, carbon steel, bronze weapons and art. The advances in metallurgy and tool-making surpassed those in Europe. Because of their deeper understanding of metallurgy,

Africans also did Iron smelting. Iron Smelting is a form of extractive metallurgy; its main use is to produce a metal from its ore.

This includes the production of silver, iron, copper and other base metals from their ores. Smelting uses heat and a chemical reducing agent to decompose the ore, driving off other elements as gasses or slag and leaving just the metal behind. Where and how iron smelting was discovered is widely debated, and remains uncertain due to the significant lack of production finds. [but] there is a further possibility of iron smelting and working in West Africa by 1200 BC. In addition, very early instances of carbon steel were found to be in production around 2000 years before the present in north-west Tanzania, based on complex preheating principles. These discoveries are Evidence that also shows that the international trade was first developed between Africa and Asia, and among these international trade relations were the exchange of ideas and cultural practices that laid the foundations of the earliest civilisations of the ancient world. And As far as the history of mining is concerned, the oldest known mine on archaeological records is the "Lion Cave" in Swaziland, which radiocarbon dating shows to be about 43,000 years old. The ancient Egyptians mined a mineral called malachite. Quarries for turquoise and copper were also found at "WadiHamamat, Tura, Aswan and various other Nubian sites".

The gold mines of Nubia were among the largest and most extensive in the world, and are described by the Greek author Diodorus Siculus. He mentions that fire-setting was one method used to break down the hard rock holding the gold. One of the complexes is shown in one of the earliest known maps. They crushed the ore and ground it to a fine powder before washing the powder for the gold dust.

Many treatments used today in modern medicine were first employed in Africa centuries ago. The earliest known surgery was performed in Egypt around 2750 B.C. Medical procedures that were Performed in ancient Africa before they were performed in Europe includes vaccination, autopsy, limb traction and broken bone setting, bullet removal, brain surgery, skin grafting, filling of dental cavities and the installation of false teeth. So when western media claims to have brought civilization to Africa it becomes a surprise because they were never better than us before colonization, but they only got better than us by enslaving us to help them be better than us, they were/are only better than us because they disturbed our history and greatness by raping our continent. The media today still portrays Africa as a place of poor people who are looking for help everywhere in the world – that is a conspiracy not only in our history but even in our image as a race; they are slowly destroying the image of Africans every single day. Several ancient African cultures birthed discoveries in astronomy. Many of these are foundations on which the world still relies on, and some were so advanced that their mode of discovery still cannot be understood.

The Dogon people of Mali amassed a wealth of detailed astronomical observations. They knew of Saturn's rings, Jupiter's moons, and the spiral structure of the Milky Way and the orbit of the Sirius star system. Many people actually dare defines colonialism as a system where foreign nationals conquer a foreign state and therefore enslave them or rule them, but it is far catastrophic than that. Colonialism has nothing to do with suppression, especially in Africa, it has nothing to do with conquering a foreign state and rule it; but on the contrary, it was about getting rid of an African man who has allowed traitors to call him a "Blackman" and that is evident because the system of colonialism is self-refuelling and regenerating to this day. I know that Adolph Hitler wanted to get rid of the Jewish race or rather exterminate them from the surface of the planet but with Africans, it was about transmuting a human being into an object or a commodity for universal trade relations between the West, America and their friends. Much evil magic and wizardry happened in this process but because a traitor cannot expose his bogus they then wrote a book of false African historical narrative to conspire against the African race that if in any way you will strive to open your eyes, all you can see is a false narrative - a deception, a lie, a manipulation, a limitation and a fiction writing that turns to look truthful to your eyes so that you can remain a slave in universal race relations and today you conform to such madness.

History need not to be a storytelling (fiction); it ought to be a reality, my friend, because a story telling is only a part of the Art & culture world not the reality of mankind. Who has written and narrated the African history that is today adopted and taught in various institutions of education in African schools? Before you answer that, do you think you will be delighted by the answer to such a humiliating reality? It is on the open that African history is written and narrated by Caucasians as adopted and taught in institutions of education in Africa and there is none, in the African Union who stand up and raise such a bubbling conflict.

If my yesterday offends my today then it means there is something wrong with my yesterday and I must do something about it.

CHAPTER THREE

UNDERSTANDING PAN AFRICANISM AND BLACK CONSCIOUSNESS

BLACK CONSCIOUSNESS and Pan Africanism have been used interchangeable by Africans who have advocated for self-awareness and self-recognition in the world that continue to look at Africans as inferior persons after the occult colonial and slave misery that occurred for over 400 years in Africa and the Diaspora. However, Pan Africanism is defined as an ideology and movement that encourages the solidarity of Africans worldwide. It is based on the belief that unity is vital to economic, social, and political progress and aims to "unify and uplift" people of African descent. The ideology asserts that the fate of all African peoples and countries are intertwined. At its core, Pan Africanism is a belief that African peoples, both on the continent and in the Diaspora share not merely a common history but a common destiny. Peter Kuryla defines Pan-Africanism as "the idea that peoples of

African descent have common interests and should be unified. Historically, Pan Africanism has often taken the shape of a political or cultural movement... In its narrowest political manifestation, Pan-Africanism envisions a unified African nation where all people of the African Diaspora can live (African Diaspora refers to the long-term historical process by which people of African descent have been scattered from their ancestral homelands to other parts of the world.)... In more general terms, Pan-Africanism is the sentiment that people of African descent have a great deal in common, a fact that deserves notice and even celebration."

So as much as Pan Africanism advocates for mainly the structural ground of Africans in political, economical, social and cultural unity and integration; Black Consciousness mainly deals with one's thinking and perception as an African (Black) person. Steve Biko defined Black Consciousness as "... an attitude of mind and a way of life, the most positive call to emanate from the black world for a long time... Being black is not a matter of pigmentation – being black is a reflection of a mental attitude. Merely, by describing yourself as black you have started on a road towards emancipation, you have committed yourself to fight against all forces that seeks to use your blackness as stamp that marks you out as a subservient being... We can see that the term black is not necessarily all-inclusive, i.e. the fact that we are all no white does not necessarily mean that we are all black. Non-whites do exist and will continue to exist for quite a longtime. If one's aspirations is the whiteness but his pigmentation makes attainment of this impossible, then that person is a non-white. Any man who calls a Whiteman "Baas", any man who serves in the police force or security branch is ipso facto a non-white. Black people – real black people – are those who can manage to hold their heads high in defiance rather than willingly surrender their souls to the Whiteman… Briefly defined, therefore, Black consciousness is the realisation by the Blackman of the need to rally with his brothers around the cause of their oppression – the blackness of their skin – and to operate as a group in order to rid themselves of the shackles that bind them to perpetual servitude. It seeks to demonstrate the lie that black is an aberration from the "normal" which is white. It is a Manifestation of a new realisation that by seeking to run away from themselves and to emulate the Whiteman, black (s) are insulting the intelligence of whoever created them black. Black Consciousness, therefore, takes cognizance of the deliberateness of the God's plan in creating black people black. It seeks to infuse the Black Community with a new-found pride in themselves, their efforts, their value systems, their culture, their religion and their outlook on life. The interrelationship between the consciousness of the self and the emancipatory programme is of paramount importance. Blacks no longer seek to reform the system because so doing implies acceptance of the major points around which the system revolves.

Blacks are out to completely transform the system and to make of it what they wish. Such a major undertaking can only be realised in an atmosphere where people are convinced of the truth inherent in their stand. Liberation, therefore, is of paramount importance in the concept of Black Consciousness for we cannot be conscious of ourselves and yet remain in bondage. We want to attain the envisioned self which is a free self." Steve Biko is one person who made the concept black consciousness known to the fullest by fashioning the Black Consciousness Movement which emanates from the ideology of Black Nationalism from our Africa in the Diaspora which was championed by Marcus Garvey and Malcolm X. Although here in Africa, Black Nationalist ideals were mainly embraced by Kwame Nkrumah who have gained low profile despite his great contribution to the Pan-African struggle worldwide. And a few years later after forming the Black Consciousness Movement (1972), Later in 1976, Biko was assassinated for no unwavering reason by the South African Apartheid government's police. A man was killed without committing a crime but rather to urge members of his race to honour and take pride in themselves by dis-complying to "White Supremacy". White supremacists and polemicists have taken a stand to eliminate Black Consciousness and Pan Africanism and they have succeeded to this day because they own the media and the educational systems and they can destroy a person's image first, before they physically kill the person so that people should feel disgusted of the person's image so that when they kill him/her, they will then behave as they have done the human family a favour. But unfortunately, they didn't destroy the Ideals of Pan Africanism and

Black Conscious because those shall forever exist in the realms of the African spirit.

However, African radicals or Pan Africanists can be dated back from the earliest day mainly from our Africa in Diaspora back in the 19th Century, around the 1800s through the contributions of Frederick Douglas (born February 1818) and much more. Frederick Douglas was an African-American social reformer, abolitionist, orator, Author and statesman who escaped from slavery to lead a movement called the abolitionist movement. The Abolitionist Movement was the movement created to end or rather abolishes slavery with the mere purpose being to end the African Slave trade and set the slaves free from their abusive and heartless slave masters who treated them like commodity in the earliest development of what is today known as "White Capital". Douglas became known for his radical oratory and anti-slavery writings. He played a major role in twisting the earliest perspectives that slaves couldn't function independently by being one of the most prominent free "Black" slaves to function so effectively in isolation from the slave master. Even many Northerners at that time couldn't believe that such a great orator had once been a slave. Without his approval, Douglas became the first African American nominated for Vice President of the United States as the running mate and Vice Presidential nominee of Victoria Woodhull, on the Equal Rights Party ticket. Doulas dedicated his entire life advocating for the extermination of slavery until his death on February 20, 1895.

But before Frederick Douglas died around 1895, the spirit of Pan Africanism, Black Nationalism and Black Consciousness gave birth to Carter Godwin Woodson on 18 December 1875. Carter G. Woodson was an African-American historian, author, journalist and the founder of the Association for the Study of African American Life and History. Woodson was one first scholar to study African-American history. A founder of The Journal of Negro History in 1915 and is believed to be the father of black history. The Journal of Negro History was targeting those responsible for the education of black children.

Through the principles, he learnt from Douglas High School between 1895-1897 he then became a teacher in different institutions of education and also became principal of Douglas High School in 1900. Convinced that the role of African American history and the history of other cultures was being ignored or misinterpreted amongst fellow scholars, Woodson saw a need for research into the neglected past of African Americans. Alongside Alexander L. Jackson, Woodson published The Education of the Negro Prior to 1861 in 1915. As a historian, Woodson believed that education and increasing social and professional contacts amongst blacks and whites could reduce racism and he promoted the organised study of African-American history partly for that purpose. Woodson later promoted the first Negro History week in Washington D.C in 1926, the forerunner of Black History Month. Carter G. Woodson is well known for his book titled "The Miseducation of a Negro" in which he believes that Africans have been taught to dishonor and discredit their own kind and it is through a re-education system that they can outthink the system of exploitation that has been designed to be self-refueling for quite a long time. In one of his books, A Century of Negro Migration, Woodson wrote: "If you can control a man's thinking, you don't have to worry about his actions. If you can determine what a man thinks you do not have to worry about what he will do. If you can make a man believe that he is an inferior, you don't have to compel him to seek an inferior status, he will do so without being told and if you can make a man believe that he is justly an outcast, you don't have to order him to the back door, he will go to the back door on his own and if there is no back door, the very nature of the man will demand that you build one."

After leaving Howard University because of differences with its president, Woodson devoted the rest of his life to historical research. He preserved the history of African Americans and accumulated a collection of thousands of artefacts and publications. He noted that African-American contributions "were overlooked, ignored, and even suppressed by the writers of history textbooks and the teachers who use them." Race prejudice, he added, "is merely the logical result of tradition, the inevitable outcome of thorough instruction to the effect that the Negro has never contributed anything to the progress of mankind." In 1926, Woodson initiated the celebration of "Negro History Week", designated for the second week in February, to coincide with marking birthdays of Abraham Lincoln and Frederick Douglas. The week of recognition became accepted and has been extended for the full month of February, now known as Black History month. Woodson died on April 3, 1950.

It is believed that the cause of his death was a heart attack. As much as the influence of the earliest African scholars grew from the United States of America, White Supremacy was shaking as the scholarly brains and Pan-Africanist thinking of Africans in the Diaspora emerges in the most intellectually appealing manner that it suppressed the methods of indoctrination and psychological brainwash. Still, in the 1800s, another giant was born on February 23, 1868 – William Edward Burghardt who became famously known as WEB Du Bois. Du Bois was an African-American sociologist, historian, civil rights activist, Pan-Africanist, author and editor. Du Bois's popularity grew when he became a leader of the Niagara Movement, a group of African-American activists who wanted equal rights for blacks. Du Bois and his supporters opposed the Atlanta compromise – an agreement crafted by Booker T. Washington which provided that Southern blacks would work and submit to white political rule, while Southern whites guaranteed that blacks would get undeveloped educational and economic prospects. Instead, Du Bois asserted on full civil rights and increased political representation, which he believed would be brought about by the African-American intellectual elite. He referred to this group as the Talented Tenth and believed that African Americans needed the odds for advanced education to develop its leadership. Du Bois was a proponent of Pan-Africanism and helped organise several Pan-African Congresses to fight for the independence of African colonies from European powers. He made several trips to Europe, Africa and Asia. It is believed that after World War I, he surveyed the experiences of American black soldiers in France and documented widespread bigotry in the United States military and he then challenged the ferocity of Racism for the rest of his life. Du Bois was a prolific author. His collection of essays, The Souls of Black Folk, was a seminal work in African-American literature; and his 1935 magnum opus Black Reconstruction in America challenged the prevailing orthodoxy that blacks were responsible for the failures of the Reconstruction Era. He wrote the first scientific treatise in sociology; and he published three autobiographies, each of which contains insightful essays on sociology, politics and history. While participating in the American Negro Academy (ANA) in 1897, Du Bois presented a paper in which he rejected Frederick Douglas's plea for black Americans to integrate into white society. He wrote: "we are Negroes, members of a vast historic race that from the very dawn of creation has slept, but half awakening in the dark forests of its African fatherland." In July 1897, Du Bois left Philadelphia and took a professorship in history and economics at the historically black Atlanta University in Georgia.

His first major academic work was his book; The Philadelphia Negro (1899), a detailed and comprehensive sociological study of the African-American people of Philadelphia, based on the fieldwork he did in 1896-1897. The work was a breakthrough in scholarship because it was the first scientific sociological study in the US and the first scientific study of African Americans. In the study, Du Bois coined the phrase "the submerged tenth" to describe the black underclass. Later in 1903, he popularised the term Talented Tenth which applied to society's elite class. Du Bois's terminology reflected his opinion that the elite of a nation, both black and white, was critical to achievements in culture and progress. Du Bois wrote in this period a dismissive way of the underclass, describing them as lazy or unreliable, but he – in contrast to other scholars, Pan Africanists and Black nationalists, attributed the societal problems to the ravages of slavery for which I believe is very true. Du Bois's contribution at Atlanta University was exceptional, despite a limited budget – He produced numerous social science papers and annually hosted the Atlanta Conference of Negro problems. Du Bois also received grants from the US government to prepare reports about African-American workforce and culture. In 1900 Du Bois attended the First Pan-African Conference, held in London from July 23 to 25. It was organised by Pan-Africanists from the Caribbean: Anténor Firmin and Bénito Sylvain from Haiti and also barrister Henry Sylvester Williams from Trinidad. Du Bois played a leading role, drafting a letter ("Address to the Nations of the World") to European leaders appeal-free the colonies in Africa and the West Indies and also to demand political and social rights for African Americans. By this time, Southern states were passing new laws and constitutions to disfranchise most African Americans, an exclusion from the political system that lasted into the 1960s. At the conclusion of the First Pan-African Conference, delegates unanimously adopted the "Address to the Nations of the World", and sent it to various heads of state where people of African descent were living and suffering oppression. The address imported the United States and the imperial European nations to acknowledge and protect the rights of people of African descent and to respect the integrity and independence of "the free Negro States of Abyssinia, Liberia, Haiti etc. W.E.B Du Bois died on August 27, 1963, in Accra, Ghana at 95.

The teachings of Pan Africanism and Black Nationalism can never be complete without the mention of Marcus Garvey; born 17 August 1887. Garvey was a Jamaican political leader, publisher, journalist, entrepreneur and orator who was a loyal protagonist of the Black Nationalism and Pan Africanism movements, in which He founded the Universal Negro Improvement Association and African Communities League (UNIA-ACL). He founded the Black Star Line, which promoted the return of the African diaspora to their ancestral lands. Garvey is mainly known for his defined Pan African philosophies – Garveyism. Garveyism intended persons of African descent in the Diaspora to redeem the nations of Africa and for the European colonial powers to leave the continent. Garvey's father had a large library, and it was from his father that he gained his love for reading.

He attended elementary education in white-owned schools where he experienced racism. In 1907, aged 20 Garvey took part in an unsuccessful printer's strike and that involvement sparked in him a passion for political/social activism. In 1910, aged 23, Garvey left Jamaica and travelled throughout the Central American region. His first stop was Costa Rica (Caribbean), where he had a maternal uncle. He lived in Costa Rica for several months and worked as a time-keeper on abanana plantation. His first debut as an editor was with a newspaper called La Nacionale in 1911. Over time, Marcus Garvey became influenced by many civil rights activist of his time, inclusive of Frederick Douglas, Carter G. Woodson, and Booker T. Washington. He ultimately combined the Economic nationalist ideas of Booker T. Washington and other Pan Africanists with the political possibilities and urban style of men and women living outside of plantation and colonial societies. After years of working in the Caribbean, Garvey left Jamaica to live in London from 1912 to 1914, where he attended Birkbeck College, taking classes in law and philosophy. He also worked for the African Times and Orient Review, published by Dusé Mohamed Ali, who was a considerable influence on him. Garvey sometimes spoke at Hyde Park's Speakers' Corner.

In 1914, Garvey returned to Jamaica, where he systematised the Universal Negro Improvement Association (UNIA). In an article titled "The Negro's Greatest Enemy", published in Current History (September 1923), Garvey explained the origin of the Organization's name: "where did the name of the organisation come from? It was while speaking to a West Indian Negro who was a passenger with me from Southampton, who was returning home to the East Indies from Basuto land with his Basuto wife, I further learned of the horrors of native life in Africa. He related to me in conversation such a horrible and pitiable tales that my heart bled within me. Retiring from the conversation to my cabin, all day and the following night I pondered over the subject of that conversation, and at midnight, lying flat on my back, the vision and the thought came to me that I should name the organisation the Universal Negro Improvement Association and African Communities (Imperial) League. Such a name I thought would embrace the purpose of all black humanity. Thus, to the world a name was born, a movement created, and a man became known." After moving to New York, he found work as a printer by day. He was influenced by Hubert Harrison. At night he would speak on street corners, much as he did in London's Hyde Park. Garvey thought that there was a leadership vacuum among African Americans. On 9 May 1916, he held his first public lecture in New York City at St Mark's Church in-the-Bowery and undertook a 38-state speaking tour. In May 1917, Garvey and thirteen other Pan Africanists formed the first UNIA division outside Jamaica. They began advancing ideas to promote social, political, and economic freedom for black people. On 08 July 1917, Garvey delivered an address, entitled "The Conspiracy of the East St. Louis Riots", at Lafayette Hall in Harlem. During the speech, he declared the riot was "one of the bloodiest outrages against mankind", condemning

America's claims to represent democracy when black people were victimized "for no other reason than they are black People seeking an Industrial chance in a country that they have labored for three hundred years to make great". It is "a time to lift one's voice against the savagery of a people who claim to be dispensers of democracy". A split occurred in the Harlem division, with Garvey enlisted to become its leader; although he technically held the same position in

Jamaica. Garvey worked to develop a programme to improve the conditions of ethnic Africans "at home and abroad" under UNIA auspices. On 17 August 1918, he began publishing the Negro World newspaper in New York, which was widely distributed. Garvey worked as an editor without pay until November 1920. He used Negro World as a platform for his views to encourage the growth of the UNIA. By June 1919, the membership of the organisation had grown to over two million, according to its records.

On 27 June 1919, the UNIA set up its first business, incorporating the Black Star Line of Delaware, with Garvey as President. By September, it acquired its first ship. Much fanfare surrounded the inspection of the SS. Yarmouth and its rechristening as the S.S. Frederick Douglas on 14 September 1919. Such a rapid accomplishment garnered attention from many. The Black Star Line also formed a fine winery, using grapes harvested only in Ethiopia. During the first year, the Black Star Line's stock sales brought in 600 000 US Dollars. This caused it to be successful during that year. It had numerous problems during the next two years: mechanical breakdowns on its ships, incompetent workers, and poor record keeping. The officers were accused of mail fraud.

Edwin P. Kilroe, Assistant District Attorney in the District's Attorney's office of the county in New York investigated the activities of the UNIA. He never filed charges against Garvey or other officers. After being called to Kilroe's office a numerous times for questioning, Garvey wrote an editorial on the assistant DA's activities for the Negro World. Kilroe had Garvey arrested and indicted for criminal libel but dismissed the Charges after Garvey published a repudiation. On 14 October 1919, Garvey received a visit in his Harlem office from George Tyler, who claimed Kilroe "had sent him" to get the leader. Tyler pulled a 38-caliber revolver and fired four shots, wounding Garvey on the right leg and the scalp. The UNIA held an International Convention in 1921 at New York's Madison Square Garden. Also represented at the convention were organisations such as the Universal Black Cross Nurses, The Black Eagle Flying Corps, and the Universal African Legion. Garvey attracted over 50 000 people to the event and in his cause. The UNIA had up to 80 000 members paying dues to his support and funding.

Garvey also established the business The Negro Factories Corporation. He planned to develop the businesses to manufacture every marketable commodity in every big US industrial centre, and in Central America, the West Indies and Africa. Related endeavours included a grocery chain, restaurant, publishing house and other businesses. Convinced that black people should have a permanent homeland in Africa, Garvey sought to develop Liberia (Land of the free, A country in the West African Coast). It has been founded by the American Colonization Society in the 19th century as a colony for free blacks from the United States. Garvey launched the Liberia programme in 1920, intended to build colleges, industrial plants, and railroads as part of an industrial base from which to operate. He abandoned the programme in the mid-20s after much opposition from European powers with interests in Liberia. In response to American suggestions that he wanted to take all ethnic Africans of the Diaspora back to Africa, he wrote, "We do not want all the Negroes in Africa. Some are no good here, and naturally will be no good there." Garvey is known as a leading political figure because of his determination to fight for the unity of African Americans by creating the Universal Negro Improvement Association and rallying to gather supporters to fight. With this group, he touched upon many topics such as education, the economy and social emancipation or independence. An important aspect of his career was his thoughts on communism. Garvey felt that communism would be more beneficial for Whites by solving their own political and economic problems, but would further limit the success of blacks rising together.

He believed that the Communist Party wanted to use the African-American vote "to smash and overthrow" the capitalistic white majority to "put their majority group or race still in power, not only as communists but as white me." The Communist Party wanted to have as many supporters as possible, even if it meant having Blacks but Garvey discouraged this. He had the idea that communists were only white men who wanted to manipulate Blacks so they could continue to have control over them. Garvey said, "It is a dangerous theory of economic and political reformation because it seeks to put government in the hands of an ignorant white mass that have not been able to destroy their natural prejudices towards Negroes and other non-white people. While it may be a good thing for them, it will be a bad thing for the Negroes who will fall under the government of the most ignorant, prejudiced class of the white race" (Nolan, 1951). As much as Garvey's popularity grew, his provocative ideas on Pan Africanism didn't only gain him support but also contempt and critiques. On 04 October 1916, The Daily Gleaner in Kingston published a letter written by Raphael Morgan, a Jamaican-American priest of the Ecumenical Patriarchate, together with over a dozen other like-minded Jamaican-Americans, who wrote in to protest against Garvey's lectures. Garvey's views on Jamaica, they felt were damaging to both the reputation of their homeland and its people, enumerating several objections to Garvey's stated preference for the prejudice of the American whites over that of English whites. Garvey's response was published a month later: he called the letter a conspiratorial fabrication meant to undermine the success and favour he had gained while in Jamaica and in the United States. At the other hand, while W.E.B Du Bois felt that the Black Star Line was original and promising, he added that "Marcus

Garvey is, without doubt, the most dangerous enemy of the Negro race in America and in the world. He is either lunatic or a traitor." Du Bois considered Garvey's programme of complete separation a capitulation to white supremacy; a tacit admission that Blacks could never be equal to Whites. Noting how popular the idea was with racist thinkers and politicians, Du Bois feared that Garvey threatened the gains made by his own movement. Garvey suspected that Du Bois was prejudiced against him because he was a Caribbean native with a dark skin. Du Bois once described Garvey as "a little, fat black man; ugly, but with intelligent eyes and a big head". Garvey called Du Bois "purely and simply a white man's nigger" and "a little Dutch, a little French, a little Negro ...a mullato ... a monstrosity". Garvey later died in 1940, leaving a worldwide recognition of the Garveyism Pan African philosophies which influenced the struggle of Black Nationalism in the Diaspora and in Africa. So as much as Garvey's life impacted many and sparked the lives of those who were moved by his teachings, his passion never died with him. On May 19, 1925, another Pan African hero from the Diaspora (US) was born – Malcolm X. Malcolm X was an orator, Black Nationalist, civil rights activist and an advocate for the Black man's social and economic status in the United States and in Africa. Malcolm X was a courageous advocate for the rights of blacks, a man who indicted White America in the harshest terms for its crimes against black Americans. Detractors accused him of preaching racism and violence. He has been called the greatest and most influential African Americans in history. Malcolm Little excelled in Junior High school but dropped out after a white teacher told him that practising law, his aspiration at the time, was "no realistic goal for a nigger". Later Malcolm X recalled feeling the white world offered no place for a career-oriented black man, regardless of talent. Malcolm X was effectively orphaned early in life. His father was killed when he was six by what he believed was the "Ku Klux Klan" and his mother suffered an emotional breakdown several years after the death of her husband and was placed in a mental hospital when he was thirteen, after which he lived in a series of foster homes. In 1946, at age 20, he was convicted of larceny and housebreaking. While in prison, he then became the member of Islam, and after his parole in 1952, he quickly rose to become one of the organisation's most influential leaders. He served as the public face of the controversial group for a dozen years.

Malcolm X was equally critical as the Civil Rights Movement. He labelled Martin Luther King Jr. a "chump" and "a religious uncle Tom" and other Civil Rights Leaders "Stooges" of the white establishment. He called the 1963 March on Washington "the farce of Washington", and said he did not know why so many black people were excited about a demonstration "run by whites in front of a statue of a president who has been dead for a hundred years and who didn't like us when he was alive". While the Civil Rights Movement fought against racial segregation, Malcolm X advocated the complete separation of African Americans from whites. He proposed that African Americans should return to Africa (their ancestral homeland) and that, meanwhile, a separate country for black people should be created. He rejected the Civil Rights's strategy of non-violence, expressing that black people should defend and advance themselves "by any means necessary". Malcolm X mentored and guided Louis X (Later Known as Louis Farrakhan), who eventually became the leader of the Nation of Islam.

The crowds and controversy surrounding Malcolm made him a media magnet. He was featured in a weeklong television programme called The Hate That Hate Produced" with Mike Wallace in 1959. The programme explored the fundamentals of the Nation of Islam, and tracked Malcolm's emergence as one of its most important leaders. After the special, Malcolm faced the uncomfortable reality that his fame has eclipsed that of his mentor, Elijah Muhammad. Besides the media, Malcolm's vivid personality had captured the government's attention. As membership in the Nation of Islam continues to grow through Malcolm X's rhetoric and programme, FBI agents infiltrated the organisation (one even acted as Malcolm X's bodyguard) and secretly placed bugs, wiretaps, cameras, and other surveillance equipment to monitor the group's activities. Malcolm's faith was dealt a crushing blow at the height of the Civil Rights Movement in 1963. He learnt that his mentor and leader, Elijah Muhamad was secretly having relations with as many as six women within the Nation of Islam organisation. As if that was not enough, Malcolm found out that some of those relationships had resulted in children. Malcolm was deeply hurt by

Muhamad'sactions because he believed that Muhamad was a living prophet. Malcolm also felt guilty about the masses he had led to join the NOI, which he now felt was a fraudulent organisation built on many too lies to ignore. On December 1, 1963, when asked for a comment about the assassination of President John F. Kennedy, Malcolm X said that it was a case "of chickens coming home to roost". He added, "Chickens coming home to roost never did make me sad; they've always made me glad." The New York Times wrote, "In further criticism of Mr Kennedy, the Muslim leader cited the murders of Patrice Lumumba, Congo leader, of Medgar Events, civil rights leader, and of the Negro girls bombed earlier this year in a Birmingham church. These, he said, were instances of other "Chickens coming to roost". The remarks prompted a widespread public outcry. The Nation of Islam, which had sent a message of condolence to the Kennedy family and ordered its ministers not to comment on the assassination, publicly censured their former shining star. Malcolm X retained his post and rank as a minister but was prohibited from public speaking for 90 days. Malcolm, however, suspected that he was silenced for another reason. In March 1964, Malcolm terminated his relationship with NOI. Unable to look past Muhammad's deception, Malcolm decided to found his own religious organisation, the Muslim Mosque. That same year, Malcolm went on a pilgrimage to Mecca, which proved to be life altering for him. For the first-time, Malcolm shared his thoughts and beliefs with different cultures and found the response to be overwhelmingly positive. When he returned, Malcolm X said that he had met "blonde-haired, blue-eyed men I could call my brothers". He returned to the United States with a new outlook on integration and a new hope for the future. This time when Malcolm spoke, instead of just preaching to African-Americans, he had a message for all races although it was in a form of advocating for the justice, freedom, equality and recognition of African Americans as human beings. Later on, he founded the Organization of the Afro-American Unity after several encounters with African leaders from Africa whom themselves had the Organization of African Unity. His political and economic philosophy were Black Nationalism and he organised a non-religious Movement that housed African-Americans from every walk of life in which he believed that religion would divide Blacks who suffered the vicious peril of the same enemy who paid no attention to their religion but their race. He said, "they don't hang you because you are Muslim, they don't hang you because you are Baptist, but they hang you because you are a Blackman in America". Malcolm X's views shaped the thinking of many and served as the Moses of those "Blacks" who could no longer wait for a prolonged process of justice, freedom and equality and continues to influence many (including me) to this day.

After Malcolm resigned his position in the Nation of Islam and renounced Elijah Muhammad, relations between the two became increasingly hot-blooded. FBI informants working undercover in the NOI warned officials that Malcolm had been marked for assassination – one undercover officer had even been ordered to help plant a bomb in Malcolm's car. After repeated attempts on his life, Malcolm rarely travelled anywhere without bodyguards. On February 14, 1965, the home where Malcolm, Betty (his wife), and their four daughters lived in East Elmhurst, New York was firebombed. Luckily, the family escaped physical injury. One week later, however, Malcolm's enemies were successful in their evil-driven agenda. At a speaking engagement in a Manhattan's Audubon Ballroom on February 21, 1965, three gunmen (blacks) rushed Malcolm onstage. They shot him 15 times at close range. The 39-year-old was pronounced dead on arrival at New York's Columbia Presbyterian Hospital. A few weeks later when Elijah Mohammad was asked to comment on Malcolm X's death on a recorded video he said with a smile and signs of satisfaction "Malcolm X preached Violence and he died violently". A man was killed for advocating for humans to be recognised as who they are – humans.

Malcolm's assassins, TalmadgeHayer, Norman 3x Butler, and Thomas 15X Johnson, were convicted of first-degree murder in March 1966. The three members were all members of the Nation of Islam. As much as the spirit of Pan Africanism and Black Nationalism grew much in our Africa in the Diaspora, Africa here gave birth to a wonderful Pan Africanist named Kwame Nkrumah, born on September 18, 1909. Kwame Nkrumah fell in love with Garveyism, he even sounded like Marcus Garvey when he speaks. Nkrumah led Ghana to independence from Britain in 1957 and served as its first prime minister and president. Nkrumah first gained power as leader of the colonial Gold Coast and held it until he was overthrown in 1966. An influential 20th Century advocate of Pan-Africanism, he was a founding member of the Organization of African Unity and was the winner of the Lenin Peace Prize in 1963. He envisioned himself as an African Lenin.

According to historian John Hedrick Clarke in his article on Nkrumah's American sojourn, "the influence of the ten years that he spent in the United States would have a lingering effect on the rest of his life." Nkrumah had sought entry to Lincoln some time before he began his studies there; on 1 March 1935, he had sent the school a letter noting that his application had been pending for more than a year. When he arrived in New York in October 1935, he travelled to Pennsylvania, where he enrolled despite lacking the funds for the full semester. However, he soon won a scholarship that provided for his tuition at Lincoln. Nevertheless, he remained short on money through his time in the United States. To make ends meet, he worked in menial jobs, including as a dishwasher. On Sundays, he visited black Presbyterian churches in Philadelphia and in New York. As a student in the United States, Nkrumah proved successful, gaining a Bachelor of Arts degree in economics and sociology in 1939. Lincoln then appointed him an assistant lecturer in philosophy, and he began to receive invitations to be a guest preacher in Presbyterian churches in both Philadelphia and New York. In 1939, Nkrumah enrolled both at Lincoln's seminary and at the Ivy League University of Pennsylvania in Philadelphia.

He gained a Bachelor of Theology degree from Lincoln in 1942, the top student in the course, and earned from Penn the following year both a Master of Arts degree in philosophy and a Master of Science in education. Nkrumah spent his summers in Harlem, a centre of black life and thought. He found housing and employment in New York City with difficulty and involved himself in the community. He spent many evenings listening to and arguing with street orators, and according to Clarke, "These evenings were a vital part of Kwame Nkrumah's American education. He was going to a university—the University of the Harlem Streets. This was no ordinary time and these street speakers were no ordinary men ...The streets of Harlem were open forums, presided over master speakers like Arthur Reed and his protege Ira Kemp. The young Carlos Cook, founder of the Garvey oriented African Pioneer Movement was on the scene, also bringing a nightly message to his street followers. Occasionally, Suji Abdul Hamid, a champion of Harlem labour, held a night rally and demanded more jobs for blacks in their own community ... This is part of the drama on the Harlem streets as the student, Kwame Nkrumah walked and watched."

Nkrumah was an activist student, organising a group of expatriate African students in Pennsylvania and building it into the African Students Association of America and Canada, becoming its president. Some members felt that the group should aspire for each colony to gain independence on its own; Nkrumah urged a Pan-African strategy. Nkrumah played a major role in the Pan-African

Conference held in New York in 1944, which urged the United States, at the end of the Second World War, to help ensure Africa became developed and free. Nkrumah read books about politics and divinity and tutored students in philosophy. In 1943 Nkrumah met Trinidadian Marxist C. L. R. James, Russian expatriate Raya Dunayevskaya, and Chinese-American Grace Lee Boggs, all of whom were members of an American-based Trotskyist intellectual cohort. Nkrumah later credited James with teaching him "how an underground movement worked". Federal Bureau of Investigation files on Nkrumah, kept from January to May 1945, identify him as a possible Communist. Nkrumah was determined to go to London, wanting to continue his education there now that the Second World War had ended. James, in a 1945 letter introducing Nkrumah to Trinidad-born George Padmore in London, wrote: "this young man is coming to you. He is not very bright, but nevertheless, do what you can for him because he's determined to throw Europeans out of Africa." Nkrumah returned to London in May 1945 and enrolled at the London School of Economics as a PhD candidate in anthropology. He withdrew after one term and the next year enrolled at University College, intending to write a philosophy dissertation on "Knowledge and Logical Positivism". His supervisor, A. J. Ayer, declined to rate Nkrumah as a "first-class philosopher", saying, "I liked him and enjoyed talking to him but he did not seem to me to have an analytical mind. He wanted answers too quickly. Part of the trouble may have been that he wasn't concentrating hard on his thesis. It was a way of marking time until the opportunity came for him to return to Ghana." Finally, Nkrumah enrolled in, but did not complete, a study in law at Gray's Inn. Nkrumah spent his time on political organising. He and Padmore were among the principal organisers of the Fifth Pan-African Congress in Manchester. The Congress elaborated a strategy for supplanting colonialism with African socialism. They agreed to pursue a federal United States of Africa, with interlocking regional organisations, governing through separate states of limited sovereignty. They planned to pursue a new African culture without tribalism, democratic within a socialist or communist system, synthesising traditional aspects with modern thinking, and for this to be achieved by nonviolent means if possible. Among those who attended the Congress were the venerable W.E.B. Dubois and some who later took leading roles in leading their nations to independence, including Hastings Banda of Nyasaland (which became Malawi) and Jomo Kenyatta of Kenya.

The Congress sought to establish on-going African activism in Britain in conjunction with the West African National Secretariat (WANS) to work towards the decolonization of Africa. Nkrumah became the secretary of WANS. In addition to seeking to organise Africans to gain their nations' freedom, Nkrumah sought to succour the many West African seamen who had been stranded, destitute, in London at the end of the war, and Established a Coloured Workers Association to empower and succor them. Both the U.S. State Department and MI5 watched Nkrumah and the WANS, focusing on their links with Communism. Nkrumah and Padmore established a group called The Circle to lead the way to West African independence and unity; the group aimed to create a Union of African Socialist Republic. A document from The Circle, setting forth that goal, was found on Nkrumah upon his arrest in Accra in 1948, and was used against him by the British authorities. The 1946 Gold Coast constitution gave Africans a majority on the Legislative Council for the first time. Seen as a major step towards self-government the new arrangement prompted the colony's first true political party, founded in August 1947, the United Gold Coast Convention. The UGCC sought self-government as quickly as possible. Since the leading members were all successful professionals, they needed to pay someone to run the party, and their choice fell on Nkrumah at the suggestion of AkoAdjei. Nkrumah hesitated, realising the UGCC was controlled by conservative interests, but decided that the new post gave him huge political opportunities, and accepted. After being questioned by British officials about his Communist affiliations, Nkrumah boarded the MV Accra at Liverpool in November 1947 for the voyage home. After brief stops in Sierra Leone, Liberia, and the Ivory Coast, he arrived in the Gold Coast, and after a brief stay and reunion with his mother in Tarkwa, began work at the party's headquarters in Saltpond on 29 December 1947. Nkrumah quickly submitted plans for branches of the UGCC to be established colony-wide, and for strikes if necessary to gain political ends. This activist stance divided the party's governing committee, which was led by J. B. Danquah. Nkrumah embarked on a tour to gain donations for the UGCC and establish new branches. Although the Gold Coast was politically more advanced than Britain's other West Africa colonies, there was considerable discontent. Post-war inflation had caused public anger at high prices, leading to a boycott of the small stores run by Arabs which began in January 1948. The cocoa bean farmers were upset because trees exhibiting swollenshoot disease, but still capable of yielding a crop, were being destroyed by the colonial authorities. There were about 63,000 ex-servicemen in the Gold Coast, many of whom had trouble obtaining employment, and felt the colonial government was doing nothing to address their grievances. Both Nkrumah and Danquah addressed a meeting of the Ex-Servicemen's Union in Accra on 20 February 1948, which was in preparation for a march to present a petition to the governor. When that demonstration took place on 28 February, there was gunfire from the British, prompting the 1948 Accra Riots, which spread throughout the country. According to Nkrumah's biographer, David Birmingham, "West Africa's erstwhile "model colony" witnessed a riot and business premises were looted. The African Revolution had begun." The government assumed that the UGCC was responsible for the unrest, and arrested six leaders, including Nkrumah and Danquah. The Big Six were initially incarcerated together in Kumasi, increasing the rift between Nkrumah and the others, who blamed him for the riots and their detention. After the British learned there were plots to storm the prison, the six were separated, with Nkrumah sent to Lawra. They were freed in April 1948. Many students and teachers had demonstrated for their release, and been suspended; Nkrumah, using his own funds, began the Ghana National College. This, among other activities, led UGCC committee members to accuse him of acting in the party's name without authority. Fearing he would harm them more outside the party than within, they agreed to make him honorary treasurer. Nkrumah's popularity, already large, was increased with his founding of the Accra Evening News, which was not a party organ but was owned by Nkrumah and others. He also founded the Committee on Youth Organization (CYO), originally intended as a youth wing for the UGCC, but which soon broke from it under the motto "Self-Government Now". The CYO united students, ex-servicemen, and even market women. Nkrumah recounted in his autobiography that he knew that a break with the UGCC was inevitable, and wanted the masses behind him when the conflict occurred. Nkrumah's appeals for "Free-Dom" appealed to the great numbers of underemployed youths who had come from the farms and villages to the towns. "Old hymn tunes were adapted to new songs of liberations which welcomed traveling orators, and especially Nkrumah himself, to mass rallies across the Gold Coast." Beginning in April 1949, there was considerable pressure on Nkrumah from his supporters to leave the UGCC and form his own party. On 12 June 1949, he announced the formation of the Convention People's Party (CPP), with the word "convention" chosen, according to Nkrumah, "to carry the masses with us". There were attempts to heal the breach with the UGCC; at one July meeting, it was agreed to reinstate Nkrumah as secretary and disband the CPP. But Nkrumah's supporters would not have it, and persuaded him to refuse the offer and remain at their head. The CPP appropriated the red cockerel as its symbol—a familiar icon for local ethnic groups, and a symbol of leadership, alertness, and masculinity. Party symbols and colours (red, white, and green) appeared on clothing, flags, vehicles, and houses. CPP operatives drove red-white-and-green vans across the country, playing music and rallying public support for the party and especially for Nkrumah. These efforts wildly succeeded, especially because previous political efforts in the Gold Coast had focused exclusively on the urban intelligentsia. The British convened a select commission of middle-class Africans, including all of the Big Six except Nkrumah, to draft a new constitution that would give Ghana more self-government. Nkrumah saw, even before the commission reported, that its recommendations would fall short of full dominion status, and organised Positive Action campaign. Nkrumah demanded a constituent assembly to write a constitution. When the governor, Charles Arden-Clarke, would not commit to this, Nkrumah called for Positive Action, with the unions beginning a general strike to begin on 8 January 1950. The strike quickly led to violence, and Nkrumah and other CPP leaders were arrested on 22 January, with the Evening News banned. Nkrumah was sentenced to three years in prison, and he was incarcerated with common criminals in Accra's Fort James. Nkrumah's assistant, Komla Agbeli Gbedemah, ran the CPP in his absence; the imprisoned leader was able to influence events through smuggled notes written on toilet paper. The British prepared for an election for the Gold Coast under their new constitution, and Nkrumah insisted that the CPP contest all seats. The situation had become calmer once Nkrumah was arrested, and the CPP and the British worked together to prepare electoral rolls. Nkrumah stood, from prison, for a directly-elected Accra seat. Gbedemah worked to set up a nationwide campaign organisation, using vans with loudspeakers to blare the party's message. The UGCC failed to set up a nationwide structure, and proved unable to take advantage of the fact that many of its opponents were in prison. In the February 1951 legislative election, the first general election to be held under universal franchise in colonial Africa, the CPP was elected in a landslide. The CPP secured 34 of the 38 seats contested on a party basis, with Nkrumah elected for his Accra constituency. The UGCC won three seats, and one was taken by an independent. Arden-Clarke saw that the only alternative to Nkrumah's freedom was the end of the constitutional experiment. Nkrumah was released from prison on 12 February, receiving a rapturous reception from his followers. The following day, Arden-Clarke sent for him and asked him to form a government. Nkrumah faced multiple challenges as he assumed office. He had never served in government, and needed to learn that art. The Gold Coast was composed of four regions, multiple former colonies amalgamated into one, and Nkrumah sought to unite them under one nationality, and bring the country to independence. Key to meeting the challenges was convincing the British that the CPP's programmes were not only practical, but inevitable, and Nkrumah and Arden-Clarke worked closely together. The governor instructed the civil service to give the fledgling government full support, and the three British members of the cabinet took care not to vote against the elected majority. Prior to the CPP taking office, British officials had prepared a ten-year plan for development. With demands for infrastructure improvements coming in from all over the colony, Nkrumah approved it in general, but halved the time to five years. The colony was in good financial shape, with reserves from years of cocoa profit held in London, and Nkrumah was able to spend freely. Modern trunk roads were built along the coast and within the interior. The rail system was modernised and expanded. Modern water and sewer systems were installed in most towns, where housing schemes were begun. A new harbour at Tema, near Accra, began to be constructed, and the existing port, at Takoradi, was expanded. An urgent programme to build and expand schools, from primary to teacher and trade training was begun. From 1951 to 1956, the number of pupils being educated at the colony's schools rose from 200,000 to 500,000. Nevertheless, the number of graduates being produced was insufficient to the burgeoning civil service's needs, and in 1953, Nkrumah announced that though Africans would be given preference, the country would be relying on expatriate European civil servants for several years. Nkrumah's initial title was Leader of Government Business in a cabinet chaired by Arden-Clarke. Quick progress was made, and in 1952, the governor withdrew from the cabinet, leaving Nkrumah as his prime minister, with the portfolios that had been reserved for expatriates going to Africans. There were accusations of corruption, and of nepotism, as officials, following African custom, attempted to benefit their extended families and their tribes. The recommendations following the 1948 riots had included elected local government rather than the existing system dominated by the Chiefs. This was uncontroversial until it became clear that it would be implemented by the CPP. That party's majority in the Legislative Assembly passed legislation in late 1951 that shifted power from the Chiefs to the chairs of the councils, though there was some local rioting as rates were imposed. Nkrumah's retitling as prime minister had not given him additional power, and he sought constitutional reform that would lead to independence. In 1952, he consulted with the visiting Colonial Secretary, Oliver Lyttelton, who indicated that Britain would look favourably on further advancement, so long as the chiefs and other stakeholders had the opportunity to express their views. Accordingly, beginning in October 1952, Nkrumah sought opinions from councils and from political parties on reform and consulted widely across the country, including with opposition groups. The result the following year was a White Paper on a new constitution, seen as a final step before independence. Published in June 1953, the constitutional proposals were accepted both by the assembly and by the British, and came into force in April of the following year. The new document provided for an assembly of 104 members, all directly elected, with an all-African cabinet responsible for the internal governing of the colony. In the election on 15 June 1954, the CPP won 71, with the regional Northern People's Party forming the official opposition. A number of opposition groups formed the National Liberation Movement. Their demands were for a federal, rather than a unitary government for an independent Gold Coast and for an upper house of parliament where chiefs and other traditional leaders could act as a counter to the CPP majority in the assembly. They drew considerable support in the Northern Territory and among the chiefs in Ashanti, who petitioned the British queen, Elizabeth II, asking for a Royal Commission into what form of government the Gold Coast should have. This was refused by her government, who in 1955 stated that such a commission should only be used if the people of the Gold Coast proved incapable of deciding their own affairs. Amid political violence, the two sides attempted to reconcile their differences, but the NLM refused to participate in any committee with a CPP majority. The traditional leaders were also incensed by a new bill that had just been enacted, which allowed minor chiefs to appeal to the government in Accra, bypassing traditional chiefly authority. The British were unwilling to leave unresolved the fundamental question as to how an independent Gold Coast should be governed, and in June 1956, the Colonial Secretary, Alan Lennox-Boyd announced that there would be another general election in the Gold Coast, and if a "reasonable majority" took the CPP's position, Britain would set a date for independence. The July 1956 election saw results almost identical to that four years previously, and on 3 August the assembly voted for independence under the name Nkrumah had proposed in April, Ghana. In September, the Colonial Office announced Independence Day would be 6 March 1957. The opposition was not satisfied with the plan for independence, and demanded that power be devolved to the regions. Discussions took place through late 1956 and into 1957. Although Nkrumah did not compromise on his insistence on a unitary state, the nation was divided into five regions, with power devolved from Accra, and the Chiefs having a role in their governments. On 21 February 1957, the British Prime Minister, Harold Macmillan, announced that Ghana would be a full member of the Commonwealth of Nations with effect from 6 March. Despite the fact that Kwame Nkrumah was the first Pan African president of the first independent African State (Ghana) he was also one of the most influential Pan-Africanists of all time. In 1962, three younger members of the CPP were brought up on charges of taking part in a plot to blow up Nkrumah's car in a motorcade. The sole evidence against the alleged plotters was that they rode in cars well behind Nkrumah's car. When the defendants were acquitted, Nkrumah sacked the chief judge of the state security court, then got the CPP-dominated parliament to pass a law allowing a new trial. At this second trial, all three men were convicted and sentenced to death, though these sentences were subsequently commuted to life imprisonment. Shortly afterward, the constitution was amended to give the president the power to summarily remove judges at all levels.

In 1964, he proposed a constitutional amendment which would make the CPP the only legal party and himself being the head. From the 60's, a worldwide surveillance over Pan Africanism began to rise as colonial powers started being terrified and amazed by the effectiveness and growth of Pan Africanists who had independent ideological superstructures as opposed to dehumanisations, indoctrination and psychological low class-alienation. On 05 December 1925, Pan Africanism and Black nationalism brought life to Robert Sobukwe. Robert Sobukwe was a South African political dissident, who founded the Pan Africanist Congress in opposition to South Africa under apartheid. In 1952 Sobukwe achieved notoriety backing the Defiance Campaign. He identified with the Africanists within the African National Congress and in 1957 left the ANC to become Editor of The Africanist newspaper in Johannesburg.

He was a strong believer in an Africanist future for South Africa and rejected any model suggesting working with anyone other than Africans, defining African as anyone who lives in and pays his allegiance to Africa and who is prepared to subject himself to African majority rule. He later left the ANC to form the Pan Africanist Congress (PAC) and was elected its first President in 1959. Robert Sobukwe became known as the Professor or 'Prof' to his close comrades and followers. This was witness to his educational achievements and powers of speech. He spoke of the need for black South Africans to "liberate themselves" without the help of non-Africans, defining non-Africans as anyone who lives in Africa or abroad Africa and who does not pay his allegiance to Africa and who is not prepared to subject himself to African majority rule.

His strong convictions and active resistance inspired many other individuals and organisations involved in the anti-apartheid movement, notably the Black Consciousness Movement.

At Fort Hare, where generations of young Black South Africans were exposed to politics, he joined the African National Congress Youth League (ANCYL) in 1948. The organisation had been established on the university campus by Godfrey Pitje, who later became its president. In 1949 Sobukwe was elected as president of the Fort Hare Students' Representative Council, where he proved himself to be a good orator. In 1950 Sobukwe was appointed as a teacher at a high school in Standerton, a position he lost when he spoke out in favour of the Defiance Campaign in 1952. He was, however, reinstated. During this period he was not directly involved with mainstream ANC activities, but still held the position of secretary of the organisation's branch in Standerton. In 1954 after moving to Johannesburg Sobukwe became a lecturer of African Studies at the University of the Witwatersrand. During his time in Johannesburg, he edited The Africanist newspaper and soon began to criticise the ANC for allowing itself to be dominated by what he termed 'liberal-left-multi-racialists'. He strongly believed in non-racialism. He was an ardent supporter of Africanist views about liberation in South Africa and rejected the idea of working with Whites. On 21 March 1960, the PAC led a nationwide protest against the hated Pass Law which requires black people to carry a passbook at all times. Sobukwe led a march to the local police station in Orlando, Soweto, in order to openly defy the laws. He was joined en route by a few followers and, after presenting his pass to a police officer, he purposely made himself guilty under the terms of the Pass Law of being present in aregion/area other than that allowed as per his papers. In a similar protest on the same day in Sharpeville, police opened fire on a crowd of PAC supporters, killing 69 in the Sharpeville Massacre.

Following Sobukwe's arrest, he was charged with and convicted of incitement, and sentenced to three years in prison. After serving his sentence, he was interned on Robben Island. The new General Law Amendment Act was passed, allowing his imprisonment to be renewed annually at the discretion of the Minister of Justice. This procedure became known as the "SobukweClause" and went on for a further three years. Sobukwe was the only person imprisoned under this clause. Sobukwe was kept in solitary confinement but permitted certain privileges including books, newspapers, civilian clothes, bread etc.

He lived in a separate area on the Island where he had no contact with other prisoners. The only contacts were his secret hand signals whilst outside for exercise. Despite this, he succeeded in giving his approval to the external PAC to adopt a Maoist political program. He studied during this time and received (among others) a degree in economics from the University of London.

It is speculated that the South African administration had profiled Robert Sobukwe as a more radical and difficult opponent than the regular ANC prisoners. Throughout his imprisonment, Sobukwe maintained communication with his friend Benjamin Pogrund who later became his biographer ("Sobukwe and Apartheid," Johannesburg, J. Ball, 1990). Sobukwe was released in 1969.

He was allowed to live in Kimberley with his family but remained under house arrest. Kimberley was suggested as an area where he could not easily foster subversive activities and also a place where he could live and work while being easily monitored by the state. He was also restricted through a banning order, which disallowed political activities. Various restrictions barred Sobukwe from travelling overseas, thus curtailing his attempts at furthering his education. For this same reason, he had to turn down several positions as a teacher at various locations in the United States. Due to lung cancer, he was hospitalised in 1977. His doctors requested that the authorities allow him freedom of Movement on humanitarian grounds. This request was refused indefinitely. He died on 27 February 1978 and was buried in Graaf-Reinet on 11 March 1978.

In 1946, the ridicule of the African race by Apartheid South Africa welcomed the birth of an Anti-Apartheid activist, Steve Biko who is well known for his Black Consciousness Movement. Biko was an anti-apartheid activist in South Africa in the 60s and 70s. Biko saw the struggle for African consciousness as having two stages, "Psychological liberation" and "Physical liberation". He later founded the Black Consciousness Movement which would empower and mobilise much of the urban black population. Since his death in police custody, he has been called a martyr of the anti-apartheid movement. While living, his writings and activism attempted to empower black people, and he was famous for his slogan "black is beautiful", which he described as meaning: "man, you are okay as you are, begin to look upon yourself as a human being". Biko was initially involved with the multiracial National Union of South African Students, but after he became convinced that Black, Indian and Coloured students needed an organization of their own, he helped found the South African Students' Organisation (SASO), whose Agenda included political self-reliance and the unification of university students in a "black consciousness."[17] In 1968 Biko was elected its first president. SASO evolved into the influential Black Consciousness Movement (BCM). Biko was also involved with the World Student Christian Federation. In the early 70s, Biko became a key figure in The Durban Moment. In 1972, he was expelled from the University of Natal because of his political activities and he became honorary president of the Black People's Convention. He was banned by the apartheid government in February 1973, meaning that he was not allowed to speak to more than one person at a time nor to speak in public, was restricted to the King William's Town magisterial district, and could not write publicly or speak with the media. It was also forbidden to quote anything he said, including speeches or simple conversations.

When Biko was banned, his movement within the country was restricted to the Eastern Cape, where he was born. After returning there, he formed a number of grassroots organisations based on the notion of self-reliance: Zanempilo, the Zimele Trust Fund (which helped support former political prisoners and their families), Njwaxa Leather-Works Project and the Ginsberg Education Fund. In spite of the repression of the apartheid government, Biko and the BCM played a significant role in organising the protests that culminated in the Soweto Uprising of 16 June 1976. In the aftermath of the uprising, which was met with a heavy hand by the security forces, the authorities began to target Biko further. On 18 August 1977, Biko was arrested at a police road-block under the Terrorism Act No 83 of 1967 and interrogated by officers of the Port Elizabeth security police including Harold Snyman and Gideon Nieuwoudt. This interrogation took place in the Police Room 619 of the Sanlam Building in Port Elizabeth. The interrogation lasted twenty-two hours and included torture and beatings resulting in a coma. He suffered a major head injury while in police custody at the Walmer Police Station, in a suburb of Port Elizabeth, and was chained to a window grille for a day. On 11 September 1977, police loaded him in the back of a Land Rover, naked and restrained in manacles, and began the 1,100 kilometres (680 mi) drive to Pretoria to take him to a prison with hospital facilities. He was nearly dead owing to the previous injuries. He died shortly after arrival at the Pretoria prison, on 12 September. The police claimed his death was the result of an extended hunger strike, but an autopsy revealed multiple bruises and abrasions and that he ultimately succumbed to a brain haemorrhage from the massive injuries to the head, which many saw as strong evidence that he had been brutally clubbed by his captors. Then Donald Woods, a journalist, editor and close friend of Biko's, along with Helen Zille, later leader of the Democratic Alliance political party, exposed the truth behind Biko's death.

During the times of Steve Biko, up in West Africa, another Pan African hero was born on 21 December 1949 – Thomas Sankara. Thomas Sankara was a Burkinabé military captain, Marxist revolutionary, pan-Africanist theorist, and President of Burkina Faso from 1983 to 1987. Viewed by supporters as a charismatic and iconic figure of revolution, he, Sankara seized power in a 1983 popularly supported coup at the age of 33, with the goal of eliminating corruption and the dominance of the former French colonial power. He immediately launched one of the most ambitious programmes for social and economic change ever attempted on the African continent. To symbolise this new autonomy and rebirth, he renamed the country from the French colonial Upper Volta to Burkina Faso ("Land of Upright Man"). His foreign policies were centred on anti-imperialism, with his government Eschewing all foreign aid, pushing for odious debt reduction, nationalising all land and mineral wealth, and averting the power and influence of the International Monetary Fund (IMF) and World Bank.

His domestic policies were focused on preventing famine with agrarian self-sufficiency and land reform, prioritising education with a nationwide literacy campaign, and promoting public health by vaccinating 2.5 million children against meningitis, yellow fever, and measles. Other components of his national agenda included planting over ten million trees to halt the growing desertification of the Sahel, doubling wheat production by redistributing land from feudal landlords to peasants, suspending rural poll taxes and domestic rents, and establishing an ambitious road and rail construction program to "tie the nation together". On the localised level Sankara also called on every village to build a medical dispensary and had over 350 communities construct schools with their own labour. Moreover, his commitment to women's rights led him to outlaw female genital mutilation, forced marriages and polygamy, while appointing women to high governmental positions and encouraging them to work outside the home and stay in school even if pregnant. Sankara is commonly referred to as "Africa's Che Guevara". In order to achieve this radical transformation of society, he increasingly exerted authoritarian control over the nation, eventually banning unions and a free press, which he believed could stand in the way of his plans.

To counter his opposition in towns and workplaces around the country, he also tried corrupt officials, "counter-revolutionaries" and "lazy workers" in Popular Revolutionary Tribunals. Additionally, as an admirer of Fidel Castro's Cuban Revolution, Sankara set up Cuban-style Committees for the Defence of the Revolution (CDRs). His revolutionary programs for African self-reliance made him an icon to many of Africa's poor. Sankara remained popular with most of his country's impoverished citizens. However, his policies alienated and antagonised the vested interests of an array of groups, which included the Small but powerful Burkinabé middle class, the tribal leaders whom he stripped of the long-held traditional right to forced labour and tribute payments, and France and its ally the Ivory Coast. He was overthrown and assassinated in a coup d'état led by Blaise Compaoré on October 15, 1987. A week before his assassination, he declared: "While revolutionaries as individuals can be murdered, you cannot kill ideas." Sankara was mainly branded for his words "Our country produces enough to feed us all. Alas, for lack of organization, we are forced to beg for food aid. It's this aid that instils in our spirits the attitude of beggars." Immediately after Sankara took office he suppressed most of the powers held by tribal chiefs in Burkina Faso. These feudal landlords were stripped of their rights to tribute payments and forced labour as well as having their land distributed amongst the peasantry. This served the dual purpose of creating a higher standard of living for the average Burkinabe as well as creating an optimal situation to induce Burkina Faso into food self-sufficiency. Within four years Burkina Faso reached food sufficiency due in large part to feudal land redistribution and series of irrigation and fertilization programs instituted by the government. During this time production of cotton and wheat shot up. While the average wheat production for the Sahel region was 1700 kg per hectare in 1986, Burkina Faso was producing 3900 kg of wheat per hectare the same year. This success meant Sankara had not only shifted his country into food self-sufficiency but had in turn created a food surplus. Sankara also emphasized the production of cotton and the need to transform the cotton produced in Burkina Faso into clothing for the people. Sankara's first priorities after taking office were feeding, housing, and giving medical care to his people who desperately needed it. Sankara launched a mass vaccination program in an attempt to irradicate polio, meningitis, and measels. In one week 2.5 million Burkinabé were vaccinated, garnering congratulations from the World Health Organization. Sankara's administration was also the first African government to publicly recognize the AIDS epidemic as a major threat to Africa. Large scale housing and infrastructure projects were also undertaken. Brick factories were created to help build houses in effort to end urban slums. In an attempt to fight deforestation. The People's Harvest of Forest Nurseries was created to supply 7,000 village nurseries, as well as organizing the planting of several million trees. All regions of the country were soon connected by a vast road and rail building program. Over 700 Kilometers of rail was laid by Burkinabé people to facilitate manganese extraction in "The Battle of the Rails" without any foreign aid or outside money. These programs were an attempt to prove that African countries can be prosperous without foreign help or aid. These revolutionary developments and national economic programs shook the foundations of the traditional economic development models imposed on Africa. Sankara also launched education programs to help combat the country's 90% illiteracy rate. These programs had some success in the first few years. However, wide scale teacher strikes coupled with Sankara's unwillingness to negotiate led to the creation of "Revolutionary Teachers". In an attempt to replace the nearly 2,500 teachers fired over a strike in 1987 anyone with a college degree was invited to teach through the revolutionary teachers program. Volunteers received a 10-day training course before being sent off to teach; the results were disastrous. Sankara's régime was criticised by Amnesty International and other international humanitarian organisations for violations of human rights, including extrajudicial executions, arbitrary detentions and torture of political opponents. The British development organisation Oxfam recorded the arrest and torture of trade union leaders in 1987. In 1984, seven individuals associated with the previous régime were accused of treason and executed after a summary trial. A teachers' strike the same year resulted in the dismissal of 2,500 teachers; thereafter, non-governmental organisations and unions were harassed or placed under the authority of the Committees for the Defence of the Revolution, branches of which were established in each workplace and which functioned as "organs of political and social control." Popular Revolutionary Tribunals, set up by the government throughout the country, placed defendants on trial for corruption, tax evasion or "counter-revolutionary" activity. Procedures in these trials, especially legal protections for the accused, did not conform to international standards. According to Christian Morrisson and Jean-Paul Azam of the Organisation for Economic Co-operation and Development, the "climate of urgency and drastic action, in which many punishments were carried out immediately against those who had the misfortune to be found guilty of unrevolutionary behaviour, bore some resemblance to what occurred in the worst days of the French Revolution, during the Terror. Although few people were killed, violence was widespread." On October 15, 1987, Sankara was killed by an armed group with twelve other officials in a coup d'état organised by his former colleague Blaise Compaoré. Deterioration in relations with neighbouring countries was one of the reasons given, with Compaoré stating that Sankara jeopardised foreign relations with former colonial power France and neighbouring Ivory Coast. Prince Johnson, a former Liberian warlord allied to Charles Taylor, told Liberia's Truth and Reconciliation Commission (TRC) that it was engineered by Charles Taylor. After the coup and although Sankara was known to be dead, some CDRs mounted an armed resistance to the army for several days. Sankara's body was dismembered and he was quickly buried in an unmarked grave, while his widow Mariam and two children fled the nation. Compaoré immediately reversed the nationalisations, overturned nearly all of Sankara's policies, re-joined the International Monetary Fund and World Bank to bring in "desperately needed" funds to restore the "shattered" economy, and ultimately spurned most of Sankara's legacy. Compaoré's dictatorship remained in power for 27 years, until it was overthrown by popular protests in 2014. Pan Africanism exist, despite the fact that Pan-Africanists are being killed for no apparent reasons, and although there may be conspiracy theories about the death of Pan-

Africans, sometimes the so-called conspiracy theories are actually the truth because our people continue to die for recognising the need to unite. One of the recent late Pan-Africanhero causing a great deal of concern and debate from Africans is Muammaral-Gadhafi, born in 1942. Commonly known as Colonel Gaddafi, Ghadafi was a Libyan revolutionary and politician who governed Libya as its primary leader from 1969 to 2011. Taking power in a coup d'etat, he ruled as Revolutionary Chairman of the Libyan Arab Republic from 1969 to 1977 and then as the "Brotherly Leader" of the Great Socialist People's Libyan Arab Jamahiriya from 1977 to 2011, when he was ousted in the Libyan Civil War. Initially developing his own variant of Arab nationalism and Arab socialism known as the Third International Theory, he later embraced Pan-Africanism and served as Chairperson of the African Union from 2009 to 2010. In 1977, Gaddafi dissolved the Republic and created a new socialist state, the Jamahiriya ("state of the masses"). Officially adopting a symbolic role in governance, he retained power as military commander-in-chief and head of the Revolutionary Committees responsible for policing and suppressing opponents. Overseeing unsuccessful border conflicts with Egypt and Chad, Gaddafi's support for foreign militants and alleged responsibility for the Lockerbie bombing led to Libya's label of "international pariah". A particularly hostile relationship developed with the United States and the United Kingdom, resulting in the 1986 U.S. bombing of Libya and United Nations-imposed economic sanctions. Rejecting his earlier ideological commitments, from 1999 Gaddafi encouraged economic privatisation and sought rapprochement with Western nations, also embracing Pan-Africanism and helping to establish the African Union. Amid the Arab

Spring, in 2011 an anti-Gaddafist uprising led by the National Transitional Council (NTC) broke out, resulting in civil war. NATO intervened militarily on the side of the NTC, bringing about the government's downfall. Retreating to Sirte, Gaddafi was captured and killed by NTC militants.

Gaddafi was a controversial and highly divisive world figure. Supporters lauded his anti-imperialist stance and his support for Pan-Africanism and Pan-Arabism, and he was decorated with various awards. Conversely, he was internationally condemned as a dictator and autocrat whose authoritarian administration violated the human rights of Libyan citizens and supported irredentist movements, tribal warfare and terrorism in many other nations. With crude oil as the country's primary export, Gaddafi sought to improve Libya's oil sector. In October 1969, he proclaimed the current trade terms unfair, benefiting foreign corporations more than the Libyan state, and by threatening to reduce production, in December Jalloud successfully increased the price of Libyan oil. In 1970, other OPEC states followed suit, leading to a global increase in the price of crude oil. The RCC followed with the Tripoli Agreement, in which they secured income tax, back-payments and better pricing from the oil corporations; these measures brought Libya an estimated $1 billion in additional revenues in its First year. Increasing state control over the oil sector, the RCC began a program of nationalisation, starting with the expropriation of British Petroleum's share of the British Petroleum-N.B. Hunt Sahir Field in December 1971. In September 1973, it was announced that all foreign oil producers active in Libya were to be nationalised. For Gaddafi, this was an important step towards socialism. It proved an economic success; while gross domestic product had been $3.8 billion in 1969, it had risen to $13.7 billion in 1974 and $24.5 billion in 1979. In turn, the Libyans' standard of life greatly improved over the first decade of Gaddafi's administration, and by 1979 the average per-capita income was at $8,170, up from $40 in 1951; this was above the average of many industrialized countries like Italy and the U.K. The RCC attempted to suppress regional and tribal affiliation, replacing it with a unified pan-Libyan identity. In doing so, they tried discrediting tribal leaders as agents of the old regime, and in August 1971 a Sabha military court tried many of them for counter-revolutionary activity. Long-standing administrative boundaries were re-drawn, crossing tribal boundaries, while pro-revolutionary modernizers replaced traditional leaders, but the communities they served often rejected them. Realising the failures of the modernizers, Gaddafi created the Arab Socialist Union (ASU), a mass mobilisation vanguard party of which he was president. The ASU recognised the RCC as its "Supreme Leading Authority", and was designed to further revolutionary enthusiasm throughout the country. The RCC implemented measures for social reform, adopting sharia as a basis. The consumption of alcohol was banned, nightclubs and Christian churches were shut down, traditional Libyan dress was encouraged, while Arabic was decreed as the only language permitted in official communications and on road signs. From 1969 to 1973, the RCC introduced social welfare programs funded with oil money, which led to house-building projects and improved healthcare and education. In doing so, they greatly expanded the public sector, providing employment for thousands. Compulsory education was expanded from 6 to 9 years old, while adult literacy programs and free university education were implemented; Beida University was founded, while Tripoli University and Benghazi University were expanded. These early social programs proved popular within Libya. This popularity was partly due to Gaddafi's personal charisma, youth and underdog status as a Bedouin, as well as his rhetoric emphasising his role as the successor to the anti-Italian fighter Omar Mukhtar. In June 1973, Gaddafi created a political ideology as a basis for the Popular Revolution. Third International Theory considered the U.S. and the Soviet Union as imperialist, thus rejected Western capitalism as well as Eastern bloc communism's atheism. In this respect, it was similar to the Three Worlds Theory developed by China's political leader, Mao Zedong. As part of this theory, Gaddafi praised nationalism as a progressive force and advocated the creation of a pan-Arab state which would lead the Islamic and Third Worlds against imperialism.

Gaddafi saw Islam as having a key role in this ideology, calling for an Islamic revival that returned to the origins of the Qur'an, rejecting scholarly interpretations and the Hadith; in doing so, he angered many Libyan clerics. During 1973 and 1974, his government deepened the legal reliance on sharia, e.g. introducing flogging as punishment for those convicted of adultery or homosexual activity. Gaddafi summarized Third International Theory in three short volumes published between 1975 and 1979, collectively known as The Green Book. Volume one was devoted to the issue of democracy, outlining the flaws of representative systems in favour of direct, participatory GPCs. The second dealt with Gaddafi's beliefs regarding socialism, while the third explored social issues regarding the family and the tribe. While the first two volumes advocated radical reform, the third adopted a socially conservative stance, proclaiming that while men and women were equal, they were biologically designed for different roles in life. During the years that followed, Gaddafi adopted quotes from The Green Book, such as "Representation is Fraud", as slogans. Meanwhile, in September 1975, Gaddafi implemented further measures to increase popular mobilization, introducing objectives to improve the relationship between the Councils and the ASU. These radical reforms led to discontent, furthered by widespread opposition to the RCC's decision to spend oil money on foreign causes. In 1974, Libya saw its first civilian attack on Gaddafi's government when a Benghazi army building was bombed. In 1975 two RCC members, Bashir Saghiral-Hawaii and Omar Mehishi, launched a failed coup against Gaddafi, and in the aftermath only five RCC members remained. This led to the RCC's official abolition in March 1977.

In September 1975, Gaddafi purged the army, arresting around 200 senior officers, and in October he founded the clandestine Office for the Security of the Revolution. In 1976, student demonstrations broke out in Tripoli and Benghazi, and were attacked by police and Gaddafist students. The RCC responded with mass arrests, and introduced compulsory national service for young people. Dissent also arose from conservative clerics and the Muslim Brotherhood, who were persecuted as anti-revolutionary. In January 1977, two dissenting students and a number of army officers were publicly hanged; Amnesty International condemned it as the first time in Gaddafist Libya that dissenters had been executed for purely political crimes. In December 1978, Gaddafi stepped down as Secretary-General of the GPC, announcing his new focus on revolutionary rather than governmental activities; this was part of his new emphasis on separating the apparatus of the revolution from the government. Although no longer in a formal governmental post, he adopted the title of "Leader of the Revolution" and continued as commander-in-chief of the armed forces. He continued exerting considerable influence over Libya, with many critics insisting that the structure of Libya's direct democracy gave him "the freedom to manipulate outcomes". Libya began to turn towards socialism. In March 1978, the government issued guidelines for housing redistribution, attempting to ensure the population that every adult Libyan-owned his own home and that nobody was enslaved to paying their rent. Most families were banned from owning more than one house, while former rental properties were seized and sold to the tenants at a heavily subsidized price. In September, Gaddafi called for the People's Committees to eliminate the "bureaucracy of the public sector" and the "dictatorship of the private sector"; the People's Committees took control of several hundred companies, converting them into worker cooperatives run by elected representatives. On 2 March 1979, the GPC announced the separation of government and revolution, the latter being represented by new Revolutionary Committees, who operated in tandem with the People's Committees in schools, universities, unions, the police force and the military. Dominated by revolutionary zealots, the Revolutionary Committees were led by Mohammad Maghgoub and a Central Coordinating Office, and met with Gaddafi annually. Publishing a weekly magazine The Green March (al-Zahf al-Akhdar), in October 1980 they took control of the press. Responsible for perpetuating revolutionary fervour, they performed ideological surveillance, later adopting a significant security role, making arrests and putting people on trial according to the "law of the revolution" (qanun al-thawra). With no legal code or safeguards, the administration of revolutionary justice was largely arbitrary and resulted in widespread abuses and the suppression of civil liberties: the "Green Terror." In 1979, the committees began the redistribution of land in the Jefara plain, continuing through 1981. In May 1980, measures to redistribute and equalize wealth were implemented; anyone with over 1000 dinar in his bank account saw that extra money expropriated. The following year, the GPC announced that the government would take control of all import, export and distribution functions, with state supermarkets replacing privately owned businesses; this led to a decline in the availability of consumer goods and the development of a thriving black market. The Jamahiriya's radical direction earned the government many enemies. In February 1978, Gaddafi discovered that his head of military intelligence was plotting to kill him, and began to increasingly entrust security to his Qaddadfa tribe. Many who had seen their wealth and property confiscated turned against the administration, and a number of western-funded opposition groups were founded by exiles. Most prominent was the National Front for the Salvation of Libya (NFSL), founded in 1981 by Mohammed Magariaf, which orchestrated militant attacks against Libya's government, while another, al-Borkan, began killing Libyan diplomats abroad. Following Gaddafi's command to kill these "stray dogs", under Colonel Younis Bilgasim's leadership, the Revolutionary Committees set up overseas branches to suppress counter-revolutionary activity, assassinating various dissidents. Although, nearby nations like Syria also used hit squads, Gaddafi was unusual in publicly bragging about his administration's use of them; in June 1980, he ordered all dissidents to return home or be "liquidated wherever you are." In 1979, the U.S. placed Libya on its list of "State Sponsors of Terrorism", while at the end of the year a demonstration torched the U.S. embassy in Tripoli in solidarity with the perpetrators of the Iran hostage crisis. The following year, Libyan fighters began intercepting U.S. fighter jets flying over the Mediterranean, signalling the collapse of relations between the two countries. Libyan relations with Lebanon and Shi'ite communities across the world also deteriorated due to the August 1978 disappearance of imam Musa al-Sadr when visiting Libya; the Lebanese accused Gaddafi of having him killed or imprisoned, a charge he denied. Relations with Syria improved, as Gaddafi and Syrian President Hafez al-Assad shared an enmity with Israel and Egypt's Sadat. In 1980, they proposed a political union, with Libya paying off Syria's £1 billion debt to the Soviet Union; although pressures led Assad to pull out, they remained allies. Another key ally was Uganda, and in 1979, Gaddafi sent 2,500 troops into Uganda to defend the regime of President Idi Amin from Tanzanian invaders. The mission failed; 400 Libyans were killed and they were forced to retreat. Gaddafi later came to regret his alliance with Amin, openly criticising him. As the 20th century came to a close, Gaddafi increasingly rejected Arab nationalism, frustrated by the failure of his Pan-Arab ideals; instead he turned to Pan-Africanism, emphasising Libya's African identity. From 1997 to 2000, Libya initiated cooperative agreements or bilateral aid arrangements with 10 African states, and in 1999 joined the Community of Sahel-Saharan States. In June 1999, Gaddafi visited Mandela in South Africa, and the following month attended the OAU summit in Algiers, calling for greater political and economic integration across the continent and advocating the foundation of a United States of Africa. He became one of the founders of the African Union (AU), initiated in July 2002 to replace the OAU; at the opening ceremonies, he proclaimed that African states should reject conditional aid from the developed world, a direct contrast to the message of South African President Thabo Mbeki. At the third AU summit, held in Libya in July 2005, he called for a greater level of integration, advocating a single AU passport, a common defence system and a single currency, utilising the slogan: "The United States of Africa is the hope." In June 2005, Libya joined the Common Market for Eastern and Southern Africa (COMESA), and in August 2008 Gaddafi was proclaimed "King of Kings" by an assembled committee of traditional African leaders. On 1 February 2009, his "coronation ceremony" was held in Addis Ababa, Ethiopia, coinciding with Gaddafi's election as AU chairman for a year. The era saw Libya's return to the international arena. In 1999, Libya began secret talks with the British government to normalise relations. In 2001, Gaddafi condemned the September 11 attacks on the U.S. by al-Qaeda, expressing sympathy with the victims and calling for Libyan involvement in the War on Terror against militant Islamism. His government continued suppressing domestic Islamism, at the same time as Gaddafi called for the wider application of sharia law. Libya also cemented connections with China and North Korea, being visited by Chinese President Jiang Zemin in April 2002. Influenced by the events of the Iraq War, in December 2003, Libya renounced its possession of weapons of mass destruction, decommissioning its chemical and nuclear weapons programs. Relations with the U.S. improved as a result, while UK Prime Minister Tony Blair met with Gaddafi in the Libyan desert in March 2004. The following month, Gaddafi travelled to the headquarters of the European Union (EU) in Brussels, signifying improved relations between Libya and the EU, the latter ending its remaining sanctions in October. In October 2010, the EU paid Libya €50 million to stop African migrants passing into Europe; Gaddafi encouraged the move, saying that it was necessary to prevent the loss of European cultural identity to a new "Black Europe". Removed from the U.S. list of state sponsors of terrorism in 2006, Gaddafi nevertheless continued his anti-western rhetoric, and at the Second Africa-South America Summit in Venezuela in September 2009, joined Venezuelan President Hugo Chávez in calling for an "anti-imperialist" front across Africa and Latin America. Gaddafi proposed the establishment of a South Atlantic Treaty Organization to rival NATO. That month he also addressed the United Nations General Assembly in New York for the first time, using it to condemn "western aggression". In Spring 2010, Gaddafi proclaimed jihad against Switzerland after Swiss police accused two of his family members of criminal activity in the country, resulting in the breakdown of bilateral relations. Libya's economy witnessed increasing privatization; although rejecting the socialist policies of nationalized industry advocated in The Green Book, government figures asserted that they were forging "people's socialism" rather than capitalism. Gaddafi welcomed these reforms, calling for wide-scale privatization in a March 2003 speech. In 2003, the oil industry was largely sold to private corporations, and by 2004, there was $40 billion of direct foreign investment in Libya, a sixfold rise over 2003. Sectors of Libya's population reacted against these reforms with public demonstrations, and in March

2006, revolutionary hard-liners took control of the GPC cabinet; although scaling back the pace of the changes, they did not halt them. In 2010, plans were announced that would have seen half the Libyan economy privatized over the following decade. While there was no accompanying political liberalization, with Gaddafi retaining predominant control, in March 2010, the government devolved further powers to the municipal councils. Rising numbers of reformist technocrats attained positions in the country's governance; best known was Gaddafi's son and heir apparent Saif al-Islam Gaddafi, who was openly critical of Libya's human rights record. He led a group who proposed the drafting of the new constitution, although it was never adopted, and in October 2009 was appointed to head the PSLC. Involved in encouraging tourism, Saif founded several privately run media channels in 2008, but after criticising the government they were nationalised in 2009. In October 2010, Gaddafi apologized to African leaders on behalf of Arab nations for their involvement in the African slave trade. Only a few towns in western Libya—such as BaniWalid, Sebha and Sirte—remained Gaddafist strongholds. Retreating to Sirte after Tripoli's fall, Gaddafi announced his willingness to negotiate for a handover to a transitional government, a suggestion rejected by the NTC. Surrounding himself with bodyguards, he continually moved residences to escape NTC shelling, devoting his days to prayer and reading the Qur'an. On 20 October, Gaddafi broke out of Sirte's District 2 in a joint civilian-military convoy, hoping to take refuge in the Jarref Valley. At around 8.30am, NATO bombers attacked, destroying at least 14 vehicles and killing at least 53. The convoy scattered, and Gaddafi and those closest to him fled to a nearby villa, which was shelled by rebel militia from Misrata. Fleeing to a construction site, Gaddafi and his inner cohort hid inside drainage pipes while his bodyguards battled the rebels; in the conflict, Gaddafi suffered head injuries from a grenade blast while defence minister Abu-Bakr YunisJabr was killed. A Misratan militia took Gaddafi prisoner, beating him, causing serious injuries; the events were filmed on a mobile phone. A video appears to picture Gaddafi being poked or stabbed in the rear end "with some kind of stick or knife." or possibly a bayonet. Pulled onto the front of a pick-up truck, he fell off as it drove away. His semi-naked, lifeless body was then placed into an ambulance and taken to Misrata; upon arrival, he was found to be dead. Official NTC accounts claimed that Gaddafi was caught in a cross-fire and died from his bullet wounds. Other eye-witness accounts claimed that rebels had fatally shot Gaddafi in the stomach; a rebel identifying himself as Senad el-Sadik el-Ureybi later claimed responsibility. Gaddafi's son Mutassim, who had also been among the convoy, was also captured, and found dead several hours later, most probably from an extrajudicial execution. Around 140 Gaddafi loyalists were rounded up from the convoy; tied up and abused, the corpses of 66 were found at the nearby Mahari Hotel, victims of extrajudicial execution. Libya's chief forensic pathologist, Dr. Othman al-Zintani, carried out the autopsies of Gaddafi, his son and Jabr in the days following their deaths; although the pathologist initially told the press that Gaddafi had died from a gunshot wound to the head, the autopsy report was not made public. On the afternoon of Gaddafi's death, NTC Prime Minister Mahmoud Jibril publicly revealed the news. Gaddafi's corpse was placed in the freezer of a local market alongside the corpses of YunisJabr and Mutassim; the bodies were publicly displayed for four days, with Libyans from all over the country coming to view them. In response to international calls, on 24 October Jibril announced that a commission would investigate Gaddafi's death. On 25 October, the NTC announced that Gaddafi had been buried at an unidentified location in the desert; Al Aan TV showed amateur video footage of the funeral. Seeking vengeance for the killing, Gaddafist sympathisers fatally wounded one of those who had captured Gaddafi, Omran Shaaban, near Bani Walid in September 2012. Gaddafi remained a controversial and divisive figure on the world stage throughout his life and after death. Supporters praised Gaddafi's administration for the creation of an almost classless society through domestic reform. They stress the regime's achievements in combating homelessness and ensuring access to food and safe drinking water. Highlighting that under Gaddafi, all Libyans enjoyed free education to a university level, they point to the dramatic rise in literacy rates after the 1969 revolution. Supporters have also applauded achievements in medical care, praising the universal free healthcare provided under the Gaddafist administration, with diseases like cholera and typhoid being contained and life expectancy raised. Biographers Blundy and Lycett believed that under the first decade of Gaddafi's leadership, life for most Libyans "undoubtedly changed for the better" as material conditions and wealth drastically improved, while Libyan studies specialist, Lillian Craig Harris, remarked that in the early years of his administration, Libya's "national wealth and international influence soared, and its national standard of living has risen dramatically." Such high standards declined during the 1980s, as a result of economic stagnation. Gaddafi claimed that his Jamahiriya was a "concrete utopia", and that he had been appointed by "popular assent", with some Islamic supporters believing that he exhibited barakah. His opposition to Western governments earned him the respect of many in the Euro-American far right. Critics labelled Gaddafi "despotic, cruel, arrogant, vain and stupid", with western governments and press presenting him as the "vicious dictator of an oppressed people". During the Reagan administration, the United States regarded him as "Public Enemy No. 1" and Reagan famously dubbed him the "mad dog of the Middle East". According to critics, the Libyan people lived in a climate of fear under Gaddafi's administration, due to his government's pervasive surveillance of civilians. Gaddafi's Libya was typically described by western commentators as "a police state". Opponents were critical of Libya's human rights abuses; according to Human Rights Watch (HRW) and others, hundreds of arrested political opponents often failed to receive a fair trial, and were sometimes subjected to torture or extrajudicial execution, most notably in the Abu Salim prison, including an alleged massacre on 29 June 1996 in which HRW estimated that 1,270 prisoners were massacred. Dissidents abroad or "stray dogs" were also publicly threatened with death and sometimes killed by government hit squads. His government's treatment of non-Arab Libyans has also came in for criticism from human rights activists, with native Berbers, Italians, Jews, refugees, and foreign workers all facing persecution in Gaddafist Libya. According to journalist Annick Cojean and psychologist Seham Sergewa, Gaddafi and senior officials raped and imprisoned hundreds or thousands of young women and reportedly raped several of his female bodyguards. Gaddafi's government was frequently criticized for not being democratic, with Freedom House consistently giving Libya under Gaddafi the "Not Free" ranking for civil liberties and political rights. That notion that we need to die for our course must be destroyed completely, why should many of our people die for a course that continues to suffer universal exploitation? Today, there is no one whom dies for their ideas to become a reality anywhere else in the world except for in Africa. There is nothing funny or glorious about the destruction of Pan Africanism through the killing of those whom believes in the advancement of African Nationalism. Something needs to be done; we need to live for our ideas to become true, what have been started in the 19th century shouldn't take much long to be executed and can be achieved in the 21st Century because that's like 200 years of Pan African defiance against the destruction of the African image by the West and America. Cowardice and pity want do us no good. We cannot continue to serve "White Supremacy" by submitting to the system of exploitation. We must embark on a programme that allows us to delineate from victimization and heal the wounds by striving for reparations. Sitting back and witness our race go down daily won't do us no good, we need to participate in every way by contributing to the well-being of our race. All these Pan Africanists included in this book shouldn't die in vain, but we must restore the moral value of our race by shackling the catastrophe of the African race's stage in the universe.

ABOUT THE AUTHOR

Vukulu Sizwe Maphindani is an Author, who has penned four books; editor, Publisher and a Black Power scholar who subscribes to MalcolmXism and Garveyism.

Born at Mninginisi Block 2, a small Village at the side of Kruger National Park; Vukulu has grown to consciousness in pain and suffering growing up at a succinctly docile and psychologically entrapped Black Society and has as such emerged as one of the most opinionated Black Power scholar in his circle. He was born at the Royal Family of Maphindani which is part of the Mdluli Clan;

the forebearing claimants of the Kruger National Park Land where his Grandfather, Ngotsa, who partnered with Ngungunyane in the 1800 century, fought the portuegese domination of the North and he owned very large Parts of Kruger Nationak Park. Vukulu is an entrepreneur who has founded Classic Age Publishing, Classic Age Castings and Classic Age Media. He completed various Youth Leadership Programmes including YALI, The Ahmed Kathrada Foundation and The Activate Leadership.

He is currently working in the programme of "Black Re-education" through Literature and one of his efforts is enclosed in the book titled The Message to a Blackman in Africa which he authored in 2012, published in 2014, 2015, revised and republished in 2016 as a second edition. He is at this point developing a central programme for the upholding of African Literature and it is evident in his fast growing independent book publishing company – Classic Age Publishing which upholds censored African literature and the emulsification of African stories which are mostly written and narrated by European and American Writers and Historians. He is a history scholar and planning to write African History, his first attempt being the capping of "True African Heroes" by writing the book titled Understanding the Mind of Malcolm X, which makes him a First South African to write about Malcolm X.

BIBLIOGRAPHIES

Congo, My Country (1962) London: Pall Mall Press. ISBN 0-269-16092-2. Foreword and notes by Colin Legum; translated by Graham Heath;

Lumumba Speaks: The Speeches and Writings of Patrice Lumumba, 1958–1961 (1972) Boston: Little, Brown and Company. ISBN 0-316-53650-4. Editor, Jean Van Lierde; translated by Helen R. Lane;

W. A. E. Skurnik, African Political Thought: Lumumba, Nkrumah, Touré (Social Science Foundation and Graduate School of International Studies, University of Denver. Monograph series in world affairs, v. 5, no. 3-4), 1968, Denver: University of Denver, ASIN B0006CNYSW;

Thomas R. Kanza, Conflict in the Congo: The Rise and Fall of Lumumba (Penguin African library), 1972, New York: Penguin, ISBN 0140410309;

Fabian, Johannes (1996). Remembering the Present: Painting and Popular History in Zaire. Berkeley: University of California Press. p. 73. ISBN 978-0520203761;

Biko, Steve (1986). I Write What I Like. San Francisco: Harper & Row. pp. 103–104;

Peter Joyce (2007). The Making of a Nation: South Africa's Road to Freedom. books.google.com. p. 142. ISBN 978-1770073128

• Thomas Sankara Speaks: The Burkina Faso Revolution, 1983–87, by Thomas Sankara, Pathfinder Press, 1988, ISBN 0-87348-527-0

Tefan Christoff. "Echoes of Revolution: Burkina Faso's Thomas Sankara." January 13, 2008Web.<http://www.dominionpaper.ca/articles/1599;

Bianco, Mirella (1975). Gadafi: Voice from the Desert. Margaret Lyle (translator). London: Longman. ISBN 0-582-78062-4;

Blundy, David; Lycett, Andrew (1987). Qaddafi and the Libyan Revolution. Boston and Toronto: Little Brown & Co. ISBN 978-0-316-10042-7;

Clarke, John Henrik, ed. (1990) [1969]. Malcolm X: The Man and His Times. Trenton, N.J.: Africa World Press. ISBN 978-0-86543-201-7;

Lomax, Louis E. (1987) [1968]. To Kill a Black Man: The Shocking Parallel in the Lives of Malcolm X and Martin Luther King Jr. Los Angeles: Holloway House. ISBN 978-0-87067-731-1;

Ghana: The Autobiography of Kwame Nkrumah (1957). ISBN 0-901787-60-4;

Douglass, Frederick. The Life and Times of Frederick Douglass: His Early Life as a Slave, His Escape from Bondage, and His Complete

History, p. 50. Dover Value Editions, Courier Dover Publications, 2003. ISBN 0-486-43170-3;

Du Bois, William Edward Burghardt. The correspondence of W. E. B. Du Bois, Volume 3.University of Massachusetts Press. p. 282. ISBN 1-55849-105-8;

Martin A. Klein, G. Wesley Johnson, Perspectives on the African past (1972);

Leverington, David (2013). Encyclopedia of the History of Astronomy and Astrophysics. New York, NY: Cambridge University Press. p. 1. ISBN 978-0-521-89994-9;

Shillington, Kevin (2005), History of Africa, p. 2. Rev. 2nd ed. New York: Palgrave Macmillan. ISBN 0-333-59957-8;

Diamond, Jared (1997), Guns, Germs, and Steel: The Fates of Human Societies, pp. 126–127. New York: W. W. Norton& Company. ISBN 0-393-03891-2;

Morgan, W. T. W. (1969), East Africa: Its Peoples and Resources, p. 18;

Nicholson, Paul T, and Ian Shaw (2000), Ancient Egyptian Materials and Technology, p. 168. Cambridge University Press. ISBN 978-0-521-45257-1